Y0-CAZ-576

EXECUTIVE

PROTECTION

A Professional's Guide to Bodyguarding

Benny Mares

Paladin Press
Boulder, Colorado

Executive Protection:
A Professional's Guide to Bodyguarding
by Benny J. Mares

Copyright © 1994 by Benny J. Mares
ISBN 0-87364-798-X
Printed in the United States of America

Published by Paladin Press, a division of
Paladin Enterprises, Inc., P.O. Box 1307,
Boulder, Colorado 80306, USA.
(303) 443-7250

Direct inquiries and/or orders to the above address.

Contents

This book is dedicated to the individuals determined to become professionals in the demanding field of executive protection.

Introduction

This book is about being a bodyguard. It describes, in depth, what is involved in becoming a member of this profession.

There are many how-to books and articles on protection and why it is necessary in today's society. This book goes a step further, covering all aspects of protecting the client: protection from others, protection from embarrassing situations, handling general emergencies in everyday life, and being prepared by anticipating potential problems—expecting the unexpected. The book describes actual circumstances, a variety of protectees, and basically what it is like actually doing the job.

As you become more interested and involved in the protection field, you will become familiar with the terminology relating to the bodyguard's role, as well as the accepted and professional titles used in the business. Many terms will be used and explained throughout this book, and there is a glossary of selected terms at the end.

The more preferred terms for bodyguard are "personal protection specialist" and "executive protection specialist." Throughout the text, I will use these inter-

1

changeably with bodyguard. Only a security professional educated and trained in executive protection deserves
to be referred to as an executive or personal protection
specialist—and knows the difference. The more you read
about the services a personal protection specialist provides beyond mere "bodyguard" protective services, the
more you will understand the differences.

The purpose of this book is not to provide you with a
single tool to open the doors to the security field. On the
contrary, it is meant to open your mind to the training
required to become a professional in this rapidly growing area.

To enter into this specialized area of security, you
must be prepared to get your hands on every available
means of assistance. You must open your mind to the
ever-changing demand of the profession and be prepared to meet every challenge.

It is unfortunate that in a country where opportunity
for growth is available in the form of so many schools,
seminars, courses and publications, we continue to
have so many organizations offering protective services
with which they are unfamiliar.

In today's society, every field has adopted a policy
whereby continued education is a prerequisite for further success. This is particularly so in the corporate
world. Since this is the world we in the security profession want to become part of, would it not be wise to
adopt our own policy of continuing education?

Executive protection involves specialized education in
areas the general "bodyguard" would not consider. This
profession is not all sunglasses, dark suits, and muscle. It
involves appropriate dress, proper etiquette in social circles, professional attitudes, speech awareness, first aid,
perceived bodyguard responsibilities, and much more. I
will deal with these points throughout the book.

The combination of proper training, experience, and
approach to your position on a protective detail will

make it harder for someone to attack your client. Instead, it will be easier for the attacker to go somewhere else, thus making your job easier. Therefore, harden the target.

Bodyguards

Bodyguard: (*n.*) A person or persons assigned to protect someone from harm.
—*Webster's New World Dictionary*

Bodyguard: (*n.*) Guard—defend, protect.
—*Webster's New World Thesaurus*

The security person uneducated in executive protection principles perceives the profession as it is defined in the dictionary and thinks, "I'm going to protect my client from any harm! I'm a bodyguard!"

By contrast, the educated professional in the business says, "I expect the unexpected, blend into the corporate and family structure, and prepare to handle every problem before it happens. I'm a personal protection specialist."

Over the past two decades, professionals have moved away from the term "bodyguard" and have begun classifying themselves and others who are well-trained in the field as executive protection and personal protection specialists.

On many occasions I have been asked what "executive protection" is. After giving a brief explanation that it is a more professional reference to, but basically a definition of, bodyguard work, I have watched an actual physical transformation take place in people. They immediately sit or stand more erect, expand their chests, and say something like, "Oh yeah, I could do that work; I work out a lot!" Or they will begin to explain how they have a relative who would be perfect for the job because he or she is in such great shape or is so big!

The general perception of a bodyguard is a huge, overbearing powerhouse who intimidates you and will cause you great pain if you fail to abide by his commands. The unskilled security person who is occasionally called for this type of protective service immediately thinks of himself as a mercenary type who must bring out the heavy body armor, load the shotgun, and carry several handguns just in case someone wants to "take out" the client.

In reality, the professional protection specialist is a capable person who blends into the circumstances and is noticed only if necessary. This agent prepares by anticipating and avoiding any problems and makes the target less vulnerable in order to make the job go more smoothly. I worked with an actor for a period of time who, after understanding the theory of "blending in," demanded that his regular bodyguards lose 20 pounds each so they would "fit his image" better.

Look at the majority of Secret Service agents and ask yourself how many of them could compete in a bodybuilding contest. Wouldn't you prefer the "average image" that blends into your business, family, or social event?

The realistic image of a bodyguard is not to be confused with the stereotypical or Hollywood perception of the typical protector. In order to have a box office hit, Hollywood must combine the highlights of several bodyguards' careers into a two-hour, action-packed drama. Unfortunately, those entering the profession believe they will be involved in such a whirlwind of activity. The truth is, very seldom, if ever, will an agent see such action. For the majority of assignments, boredom is the rule—and as long as there is boredom, the bodyguard is doing the job successfully.

I do not mean to imply that this profession is boring. In fact, the opposite is true. I know of no other career that allows you to travel first class, stay in the best of hotels, dine in the finest restaurants, and get paid well as you see the world. The opportunities are endless, but the "shoot 'em up, punch 'em out" action-filled scenes are very rare.

As we progress, you will begin to understand that the more action you find, the more liability you expose your client to. Therefore, there are certain qualities, skills, and areas of education that will enable you to be a true professional and *avoid* a particular type of action. Self-discipline, excellent physical conditioning, willingness to be a team player and good mental attitude are qualities that are essential in a bodyguard.

The fact that many assignments involve working alone dictates the need for self-discipline. In such situations, *you* make the decisions and *you* set the plans into action. As you become more experienced you will be assigned as the team leader, making decisions and plans for the whole team. Additionally, as a member of the team, you must be a team player. You must be able to get along well with others for the success of the team as well as the protection of the client.

To be up to both the variety of assignments and the tedium, you must be in excellent condition and maintain a proper mental attitude. You will receive detail assignments that include all the activities you can imagine, and the clients will expect you to participate. I have been involved with principals (clients) whose activities included water sports, jogging, soccer, football, horseback riding, motorcycles, and weight lifting.

Again, let me emphasize the importance of taking part in the activities—one, the client likes you to participate, and two (most importantly), you have to be with him to protect him.

The most important skills you must possess are a working knowledge of unarmed combat and a thorough understanding of weapons. Many people profess that a formal background in law enforcement, military, or some related government agency is required. I believe that experience in one of these areas is helpful but not mandatory. Even where executive protection is a part of an agency's training, it differs from methods used in the private sector.

Although one need not be a black belt in the martial arts, knowing the basics of close, unarmed combat is essential. This is the skill most called upon, as you are generally positioned near the principal. Should someone attempt to attack your client, grope excessively in admiration, or merely stumble toward him in a drunken state, you need to know how to combat each situation without drawing attention to your detail.

As for armed combat, most of the professionals I know are not strong advocates of carrying a weapon on a detail. The basis for this stems from the fact that, believe it or not, there is very little need for a weapon. I have been asked many times, "What do you do about weapons when you go to other countries, or from state to state?" In other countries I do not carry a weapon because the laws vary widely, and most of the time local agents support the team. The same generally applies in different states. As a retired police officer who served 20 years with the Los Angeles Police Department (LAPD), I know whereof I speak when I say that not every state or city recognizes the right to carry a concealed weapon.

Another critical point in polishing the attributes of a professional protector is education. One must keep an open mind to the necessary areas of education, and first and foremost is taking a course in executive protection offered by a reputable training facility (ask around, seek references). These are the true professionals that will guide you through the basics and direct you toward all advanced studies.

Now, an important concern of everyone serious about entering this profession is how to differentiate between a good training facility and a "fly-by-night" organization that merely wants to cash in on the demand for bodyguards. This *should* be a concern, as the sham artists create a negative impression of even the true professionals.

There are several great schools that provide the basic essentials of the profession (see "Executive Protection Training Facilites at the back of this book). Don't be shy about asking questions when investigating the company offering the training: How long has the school been in existence? Who are the instructors? Where do the instructors work? Can you get references?

One school, often referred to as the "best of the best," has about 20 instructors, provides more than 100 hours of training in six days, and the "details" involve activities throughout four states. Another very reputable five-day course offers training by an organization that specializes in providing executive protection personnel worldwide. All instructors are active personal protection specialists.

There are also many fine "teaser" courses available to give you an introduction into the business. Many companies train their own agents as a prerequisite to a bodyguard assignment. But be aware, don't become a victim of "Smokescreen Security," advertising "the finest personal protection agents available" and anointing inexperienced uniformed guards to answer the call for bodyguard services. This is a dead-end street. A true professional reads between the lines of such references. Ask questions. Speak with the agents. The reputable companies will not be offended by your requests; on the contrary, they will favor your questions and discussions.

The tuition for these schools is not cheap. The price varies, from an average of $100 per day for the introductory seminars to several thousand dollars per week for participation in the more in-depth schools. However, don't base your decision on price alone. Investigate quality. (Note: A good teaser course will encourage you to follow up in the more advanced training facilities.)

Most schools will either include a hands-on seminar on defensive driving as part of their curriculum or direct you to a separate course that covers this vital area. A personal protection specialist must have a thorough understanding of the principles and practices of evasive driving as they are used in this profession. Because so much time is spent in a vehicle, and driving may be your assignment, it is absolutely critical that you be proficient at evasive driving tactics.

Defensive driving strategies consist of tactics designed to assist the bodyguard in protecting the client. These techniques include using the driver and vehicle to cover the client and evacuate from dangerous situations. Such situations may involve an ambush; therefore, knowledge of how to avoid the confrontation may be the difference between life and death.

The following hypothetical situation illustrates the importance of this training. Upon approaching a vehicular barricade, you must make a split-second decision: Do you reverse your direction or go through the roadblock? Reversing the car's direction, almost instantaneously, involves one of two methods: a "J" turn or a "bootleg" maneuver. Going through involves a specialized ramming technique. These and many other tactics are taught in defensive driving courses.

Good schools place similar importance on providing an education in terrorist and criminal mentalities. Every reputable school will provide a thorough overview of terrorism, as terrorist activities often provide the rationale for commissioning the services of bodyguards. The ability to understand the mentality of terrorists will enable you to properly prepare your defenses by combating their strategies.

There are many sources for an education in terrorism. Begin your research with minority group organizations such as the Anti-Defamation League of B'nai B'rith and the NAACP. Check the current affairs and radical groups sections of your local bookstore, get back issues of monthly security magazines, and, of course, check the library.

Any public library should have a computer reference source called "Info-trac" that will list numerous publications relating to terrorism. If you have access to this source, begin your research with "Terror." My library's system cross-referenced more than 60 titles. I would recommend you read two books initially: *The Terrorism Reader* and *The Never-Ending War* (see "Recommended Reading" at the back of this book).

A word of caution: proceed slowly. Don't try to absorb the entire terrorist network overnight. You cannot "cram" to become an expert in terrorism. Be aware of the burnout factor. I thoroughly enjoyed the study of terrorism by easing into it. A comfortable method of study is to select a group based on its ethnic roots or its activities throughout the world. After completely understanding one group's beliefs and methods, tackle a new group.

Within a year or two, you will have a working knowledge of many organizations and will be comfortable discussing the field of terrorism. Most importantly, you will know the origin of threats against various ethnic or racial clients and will be more prepared to protect them.

Last but definitely not least is gaining a working knowledge of emergency medical procedures. Learn CPR, first aid, and all aspects of general emergency care. Know enough to render aid until medical professionals arrive. This area of expertise will come into play more often than you expect, so expect it and be prepared.

Those are the necessary skills, qualities, and attributes that will allow you to enter into one of the most exciting and fastest-growing professions in the world. Those of us in the profession have maintained for many years that when terrorism hits U.S. soil, there will be a much greater demand for qualified agents. This belief has been verified since the bombing of the World Trade Center in New York on February 26, 1993. On that day, I was going through customs at JFK International Airport in New York after returning from a detail throughout Europe and the Middle East. Upon hearing the news, I remember saying to myself, "It (terrorism) has hit America, executive protection will skyrocket." There has been a substantial increase in the demand for services and interest in the business since then.

There are many areas within the United States that are considered virgin territory for executive protection services. It is no longer necessary to focus only on New York, Washington, D.C., and Los Angeles. There is still time to "get in on the ground floor" in this field.

Clientele

Being a bodyguard involves working with a wide variety of clients. The more notable and expected protectees are celebrities, corporate executives, and the rich and famous. However, it is unlikely in the initial phase of your career that you will be assigned to such clients, except perhaps for positions that are outside their inner circle.

Consider yourself fortunate if your first few assignments involve clients who meet your expectations with regard to what a bodyguard detail will involve. Strong words of caution are necessary at this point. Do not get discouraged if the first jobs are not quite what you expect. These initial assignments will generally involve stationary positions, such as protecting the perimeter in the backyard, at a gate, possibly at an exit during a party, inside a home, or in hallways near an elevator or fire exit. In other words, you will be protecting areas near the client, but you will not be with him. The more experienced agents will move with the protectee. However, be extra alert and provide the client with the protective service he or she expects. The other agents will notice you in the course of their movements, and you will have the opportunity to observe and learn from them. As your experience expands, so will the requests for you to be a member of the moving part of the team.

Many requests for protection are from attorneys for their clients, as a result of threats, abusive letters, and annoying phone calls. I recall receiving one such call from a corporate lawyer who needed protection for an employee who was the victim of an attempted rape while on the corporation's property. We provided a female agent to pose as a visiting cousin. The agent lived with the family for a few weeks and provided the lady with a ride to and from work each day. The "cousins" enjoyed each other's company until the attacker was caught.

Clients come from every imaginable occupation, country, and position in life. Once you have completely entered the profession—and by this I mean you are not just called upon by a company when a certain family comes to town or when a particular executive plans his travel, but you are recognized as having the ability to provide complete services—then you will realize the unlimited source of clients.

Throughout the book I will be stressing the importance of "blending in with your client's surroundings" (i.e., becoming a part of the corporate or family structure) when providing professional protection.

It is necessary to have a knowledge of typical clients to give you an idea of where your expectations should start and thus a base to expand from. Clients who require protection from the private sector on a regular basis are corporate executives, celebrities, rock stars, authors, models, foreign dignitaries and executives (those not afforded Secret Service protection), strike personnel, and members of many ruling Arab families. Politicians are regularly provided protection by state or government agencies.

Corporate executives call for any number of concerns.

With each request for services, your challenge will be how to "blend in" effectively to provide the highest protection with the fewest problems. One assignment I had was with a female executive conducting a corporate takeover. Her job was to assemble 62 executives from the corporation being taken over into a room for a conference. The participants believed it was a meeting to discuss their roles in building the new organization, when actually this was the group being terminated on the spot! My job was to prevent any potential harm to my principal.

In a corporate takeover, all of the executives involved are not necessarily familiar with each other, as the corporation will generally include several different company branches. After advising my client that I would "blend in" with the executives in the front row, I sat in the aisle seat waiting for her speech and the unfortunate announcement. When she "dropped the bomb" on them, many became irate and boisterous. One man ran forward to confront my client. I rose, stood in the aisle facing my client, violently cursing her actions and decisions, while effectively blocking this irate former employee. All the commotion allowed my client an easy opportunity to slip out the back. No one knew any different, and no major problems occurred.

The lesson here is one of blending in with the corporate setting and improvising to provide the protection. The strong image of security is not always necessary, and many times the opposite is better. Direct confrontation may result in unwanted liability problems. The more professional your services are, the wider your client base will be and the more often your phone will ring.

In the corporate world, requests for protective services are primarily for male clients, only because of the ratio of men to women executives. However, this ratio is changing. Do not assume that a corporate call means your client will be male. Also, be aware that the families of executives are regularly included as principals.

Foreign dignitaries and celebrity protectees can be of any sex and any age. If you have difficulty working with—or for—women or children, I would advise you to consider this aspect of the security profession carefully. Years of experience with a wide range of clients are required before you reach the level of being able to select your clients. In the meantime, your clientele will be male and female and will include children of all ages.

Things are also changing with regard to the client's preference for agents. Because of the original perception of a bodyguard as a bulging hulk shielding the client from everyone like an NFL lineman, most clients have traditionally preferred male agents. Fortunately, the current trend is for clients to consider the education and experience of an agent and not merely the gender.

Many details will involve protecting a male and female, be they husband and wife, business associates, or a couple together for any number of reasons. This type of assignment is a natural for a "double date" with a male and female agent. I recall one such request for protection from a well-known international star who was taking his wife to an amusement park. I assigned a couple as their agents. Prior to their day at the park, I received a call from the star's publicity person, who informed me that a female had never been assigned before and he was sure it would be inadvisable this time. After a lengthy discussion on the professional reasons for my decision—highlighting the importance of blending in and the fact that this client's wife had a fetish for wild hats that could, for instance, be grabbed and shredded in a ladies room before a male could respond—he allowed the couple to continue the assignment.

This particular client had a policy of tipping every night at the end of a detail. At the end of the outing, the female agent received twice as much money as her male counterpart. The client expressed his satisfaction with her abilities, and the "double date" was established as proper procedure.

My experience has shown that details involving Middle Eastern executives, royalty, and their wives and children are most often handled by male agents, as demanded by the clients. The exceptions are hallways, perimeter, and other obscure positions. It will probably be a while before this base of clientele adjusts its attitudes and begins hiring security based on qualifications rather than gender, due to the fact that Middle Eastern society is still based on the premise of male dominance. Overall, however, this is a relatively small and seasonal group of clients, and with the rapid growth of this profession, the need for qualified agents, both male and female, remains high.

A quick word on working with children. When assigned to a small child, you can take two approaches—that of doing only a security job, just watching the child at play and expecting his nanny to make sure they do not fall or otherwise get hurt, or a closer and more interactive one of playing with the child as you would your own. Either way is acceptable; however, on initial assignments, I have found the latter approach results in more requests from everyone that you be assigned on the next visit.

With older children, especially teenagers, your function consists more of observing. The main goal with this age group is to establish a clear understanding that you are in charge. What the parents want or what you decide is best for safety will always be the rule of the day.

At this point, let me advise you that there will be times when you have to ask yourself, "Where do I draw the line?" In this profession it must be understood that celebrities, royalty, and many VIPs have been accustomed to having everything at their fingertips—regardless of their desires or fantasies, it's instantly available. Many tire of the more readily available pleasures and seek satisfaction by exploring other avenues. These attractions may involve drugs and prostitutes or other controversial avenues.

Now that I've got your attention, make no mistake—this is where you have to make a decision! Do you draw the line at certain activities or look the other way? Your decision will be the primary factor in determining the clientele you are assigned to protect.

My personal advice? I've always made it a solid practice to remain above-board when it comes to anything controversial. In other words, do not get involved in activities that will cause embarrassment to your client or require you to cover for the client.

It is no secret that some young Saudi Arabian princes seek the favors of high-class prostitutes. Their entourages always include "arrangers" for these services—more commonly known as "pimps." Many times they ask their bodyguards if they have any "connections." Don't fall into this trap! Once you have crossed the line, you have lost their respect and are considered expendable. They will consider you someone who will do anything to remain in their good graces. Guard your professionalism. You are there to protect your clients, not provide for them.

Keep in mind that once you have drawn the line, they will respect you for your professionalism and for the services you were hired to provide. Yes, the pleasure-seeking activities will still go on; however, you will not be assigned during these times. Others in the group will watch the client. The activities will not be mentioned in your presence. This shows respect for your professionalism.

A final word of caution. Some illegal actions, such as drugs or child pornography, can result in everyone in the group's being suspect, regardless of knowledge or participation. So the decision of whether or not to protect certain clients who are involved in controversial activities, be it based on legality or morality, is yours alone. The bottom line is professionalism. No matter where you are assigned or who your clients are, the more professional you are, the more active you will be.

The Detail 3

The detail must always begin with a team briefing. This is critical, whether it's a team that has protected this same group of clients before or it's a new group of agents. During the briefing, modifications are made to the itinerary, certain topics are reviewed, and each agent's position is assigned.

A briefing will cover, among many other things, the principal's identity and his itinerary, the threat level and basis for it, the general hours of assignments, ground rules for the detail, the expected length of the detail, involvement of outside persons or agencies, and the site of the command post. The briefing is the first formal step toward putting your mind in gear for the job.

Every detail demands mental alertness, physical fitness, and complete professionalism in your performance. Many, if not most, assignments call for a very casual approach. The major variation, of course, would be the high-profile detail. Therefore, I will break down the general areas you can expect to work on an assignment and point out the areas that involve greater vulnerabilities and require increased awareness.

As inadvisable as a one-man detail is, you will receive requests or assignments for them. Whether you accept such a position is entirely your choice. My advice is that you determine the threat level before making your decision. Many of the very rich have only one agent with them as they go about their everyday activities. Also, when a company puts together a large detail, the individual assignments regularly involve working alone with a principal. But keep in mind that it is a completely different game when the threat level is high.

As I mentioned earlier, on your initial assignments upon entering this field, you should expect to find yourself positioned outside the principal's room, most likely near an elevator, guarding a hallway for a 12-hour shift, or manning a post within the perimeter of the main location being protected. It is also common to be assigned to perform the dual duties of driving and providing executive protection. However, driving demands your attention to the road, traffic, and so many other safety concerns for the principal that it detracts from the primary responsibilities of a personal protection specialist. Unless you are just being assigned to drive for an errand or because it is a real and unforeseen necessity, advise the client that, regardless of the threat level, a dual assignment of driver and protector would compromise the effectiveness of either position in an emergency.

Again, most details involve assuming a relaxed appearance and allowing the principal to conduct business or social activities without a feeling of being restrained. A primary reason executives get rid of personal security is that they feel their movements are restricted. In other words, they are falling all over the agents because the agents feel they are doing a better job if they are within arm's reach of their clients.

Now just the opposite is true when the executive can move freely in any environment, knowing the agents are watching him and will react if necessary. Provided this level of space and comfort, the principal will view the security team as a vital part of his budget and lifestyle. So rule number one on a detail is *never inhibit or challenge a client's movements unless absolutely necessary and critical.*

Always be aware of your surroundings. A good advance (i.e., a careful analysis of everything ahead of schedule) can enhance your knowledge of the areas and activities of interest, provide necessary contacts, and minimize problems. As we move into the general areas where your activities will take place, remember that during a detail you may not always have an opportunity to do an advance. That is why making personal contacts and even doing advances on your own time will benefit you and enhance the quality of your services to a higher level than that of your competition. So, as the Boy Scouts are taught, *always be prepared.* (Advances are covered in depth in the "Expect the Unexpected" chapter.)

No matter where the detail takes you, the following are the majority of areas you should become familiar with. I have included some experiences that will benefit you in making the assignment successful.

AIRPORTS

As an executive protection specialist, you will be dealing with your client on private airport terminals on most occasions. When the corporate executive arrives by commercial airlines, airport knowledge can make an arrival or departure a smooth, uneventful experience.

Do not panic because you see so many people running and maneuvering around others. This is natural in an airport. People are always in a hurry. Do not think you have to block for your principal. Just be aware and watch people's eyes and facial expressions as they get near your client. Watch their hands and body movements as they approach. This may seem difficult at first, but it becomes second nature. You learn to scan every-thing and everyone quickly without being obvious, and you will have plenty of time to react if necessary.

The higher the threat level, the less likely it is that a client will arrive by commercial airlines. Therefore, at a public airport, the focus should be on delays, parking, luggage, and matters that would be likely to cause embarrassment as opposed to danger.

On more than one occasion, even though I had called ahead, I arrived at an airport to find that the scheduled flight was delayed. Such a situation could cause unnecessary embarrassment if your employer had to wait in the main terminal for any length of time. After a principal gets accustomed to his security team doing everything for him, he expects you to fix every-thing, so be ready to move in every direction to provide your client with the comfort and facilities he expects.

If a plane is delayed, or for some reason transporta-tion from the airport is held up, arrange for your client to get the VIP treatment in one of the airline VIP rooms. This is not as easy as it sounds, especially if the client is not a member of any club. This is another area where advance work will show your professionalism. On your own time, visit the various VIP rooms. Introduce yourself to the personnel, especially the managers and executives, and briefly explain the pro-fession and your responsibilities to your clients. (Proper attire is critical. See "Etiquette, Dining, and Dress".) Inquire as to the availability of courtesy pass-es, explaining that possibility of your clients' needing to use such a pass is remote but describing, if neces-sary, the embarrassment that would ensue if they were without one. Advise your contacts that in the event of a visit by any of your clients, you will encourage them to join the VIP club. If you find that you cannot be accommodated, consider joining a club as a necessary investment. The membership fees average $100 per year. It has been my experience that a proper presentation of the need, a humble attitude, and a professional appearance work wonders. Most clubs will extend courtesy visits, as they know the caliber of persons frequenting their rooms.

Another consideration is maintaining very good radio contact with your driver to ensure that the vehicle is waiting directly in front of the terminal as you exit. As every airport enforces its "no parking—loading and unloading zone only" laws, proper radio contact and good public relations with the airport traffic officers are essential to effecting a smooth transition from an airport.

HOTELS

Arriving at a hotel can be quite an experience, depending upon your client. A corporate executive's arrival should consist of a normal entrance, i.e., out of the car and straight to the room. (All check-ins should be done in advance). The higher your client's status, the more ceremony the hotel will put into welcoming the guest. A royal family will be met at the entrance by most of the hotel staff, especially the manager, concierge, and food service manager.

Working a hotel detail—which will include not only the one you are staying in but all those the principal visits—can be the most casual part of the assignment. When the client is in the room there is a waiting period until you are called, and unless you have been discharged for the evening, you do nothing but wait for the call to action. The other areas principals frequent in a hotel are the lobby, restaurants, and bar areas. Your responsibility during these visits will be to act normal and do as the client does. If the client is standing around or sitting, you do the same at a distance. Advise servers in bars or restaurants that you are security for the client and that your bill should be included with his. Request that they serve you first if possible. This allows you to finish and be ready to move quickly.

I have never worked a detail where the procedure differed from this, unless the client was not dining with any business associates or guests, in which case I would be asked to join his or her table.

In keeping with the rule of always being aware of your surroundings, make sure you are familiar with all accesses to routes of escape in case of an emergency, and also be aware of anyone paying an inordinate amount of attention to your client.

RESTAURANTS

Most clients know the necessity of making reservations in advance. This is the preferred procedure of most of the finer dining establishments. On several details working with a Saudi Arabian princess, I was required to call from the vehicle for reservations as the princess decided where to dine.

Royalty does not like to wait, so again, tact and public relations must become an integral part of your personality and your arsenal of weapons. Upon receiving notification from the principal, call the restaurant and speak to the person in charge at that time. Many agents will panic and try to demand that a table be waiting because they are "representing a VIP." Obviously, this sort of arrogance creates an offensive first impression. Bear in mind that the restaurant representative has the ability to refuse you for any reason. In such a situation, it pays to be sincere and honest. Explain your position, who your client is, and that any cooperation the restaurant's management can provide will be greatly appreciated, which you will of course demonstrate by taking care of everyone involved in assisting you.

I worked a six-week detail with a princess that operated this way every day and in several cities. The only inconvenience we experienced was when the restaurant representative explained there would be a short delay, never more than 30 minutes, but that we would be accommodated. At that point I merely explained to the principal that everything was taken care of, but because of the short delay, we would have to cruise the city for awhile.

It makes a great impression when you call, receive the all-clear notice that your tables are waiting, drive up, and escort your client directly to the table.

In the event that the restaurant can only provide one table, take it! Ask them to provide for security as soon as possible, but accommodate the client. Under these circumstances, you would wait at the bar with your cola or ice tea. Now, depending on the level of threat to your client, eye contact with the principal may be either crucial or unnecessary. In the event that you must keep your client in view but the bar is situated in such a way that you cannot, be innovative. This would not be the time to play mysterious with the restaurant personnel. Explain your position and the necessity of your being in close proximity to your client. Many times I have stood in kitchens that offered a view from the window in the door, near coffee stands, and in coat rooms. On one occasion, I stood in the disc jockey booth overlooking the capacity-filled lounge as I communicated to an agent positioned nearer to the protectee.

Upon being seated, order something that can be served quickly. Remember, you are finished when the client gets up to leave. In keeping with your earlier assurance that everyone would be taken care of, you must often advise the servers to add a 30-percent service charge to the bill. (In most countries the tip is added automatically; therefore, foreign dignitaries regularly pay only what is presented to them, never intentionally meaning to offend anyone.) The generous amount of gratuity will be remembered and will encourage the management and staff to make every effort to assist you in the future.

Most clients will agree to a 25- to 30-percent gratuity.

When you are working with celebrities, always try to get a table as near to them as possible. Immediately upon receiving your assignment, determine their normal procedure with regard to being approached for autographs, photos, or mere conversation.

Most celebrities prefer not to be disturbed during dinner but will make an effort to acknowledge their fans afterward or at other times. One method I always suggest that clients use in lieu of signing autographs on the spot and stopping for photos is for them to say hello to fans and allow me to take their names and addresses so that an autographed photo could be sent to them. I find that many stars prefer this procedure, as it allows them a greater amount of freedom and provides the fans with more than they had expected. The autographed photo promise also works wonders when you're asking for small favors in your advances and regular detail work.

Although the photo promise may add extra work for you, it is a great convenience for your client. If you intend to use this tactic, make and keep a very important promise to yourself—never forget to follow up with the promised photo. Most of the time you can give the fans' names to the public relations director, but remember, *you* made the promise—be sure it is upheld.

SHOPPING MALLS

Working a detail in a mall is probably the most casual part of any assignment you will ever receive. Shopping is a very relaxed activity, so accept it and merely watch the client the way you would watch your own family, except from a distance.

An important aspect of shopping when you are protecting a member the opposite sex is allowing the client a greater amount of space. This applies especially when a female protectee is shopping for clothing or personal items.

In a department store, as long as you have your client's activities in sight, you can maintain a much greater distance. The main areas to be aware of are the exits from the sections your client is in.

When the client is in a small store where the front area is the only public entrance and exit, you can wait just inside or even outside of the store. By maintaining visual contact, you will know when your client is at the register or approaching the front. Then you very casually enter into the stream of shoppers and resume your protection.

After a period of time, you can generally get a feel for the clients' shopping methods, likes, and dislikes, and will be able to anticipate some of their movements (*generally* is the key word here; be advised that you should always expect the unexpected).

Once, on a three-man detail in a large Beverly Hills mall, my associates and I were each positioned at distances to cover any direction our two lady clients chose to move in. I overheard the clients refer to a shop they were looking for that was on the next level up. Knowing there should always be a "point-man" (the agent assigned to protect the client from any harm originating from the front of the detail) going up or down an escalator, I moved to the escalator. I was halfway up the escalator when I casually looked back and observed my teammate giving me hand signals that indicated the clients had changed their minds and were taking the elevator to a lower level. Fortunately, I was aware of my surroundings and was able to catch up with the team by the time they exited the elevator.

THEATERS

Movies make for an enjoyable part of an assignment if you enjoy them, but be aware that your job is to protect the client. This is not to imply that you cannot watch the film but to remind you to watch your client's movements as well. The principal may get up to go to the rest room, smoke in the lobby, decide he or she does not care for the movie, or leave for any reason. Be prepared to move immediately. This basic principle applies to any theater, concert hall, or confined area.

Theater managers are accustomed to having celebrities and VIPs visit their establishments, and they always seem willing to accommodate a detail when requests are within their means. Wherever there is a balcony or special seating available, I ask to speak to the manager, explain my position, and request that area for the detail. Even if the area is closed, theater managers will generally grant such special requests.

Concerts are completely different with regard to the assigned seating and the attending crowds. There is a wide variety of protective rules, depending upon the age group of fans attending, the artist performing, and the popularity of the performer. I have seldom had a problem with the seating, but always insist on seats next to or in back of the client. Working in crowded facilities demands that you have radio contact with other agents and especially your drivers. If you are in a symphony or other special concert and the client needs you to "blend in," then advise others outside of the concert to listen for *your* radio contact because you will be off the air. The reason for this is that your radio or earpiece would draw unnecessary attention to your detail.

CLUBS

When you are part of a detail that is protecting a client who is a member of a private club, you can expect very few problems because the clientele usually consists of regulars or VIP's and celebrities are expected to be in the club.

If a visiting dignitary wants to check out a private club, then your skills, personality, and limits of gratuities come into play. This is when an advance is absolutely necessary. Most managers work with team leaders and fulfill special requests. I have found this true in most every country.

Nightclub activity is the same in any setting. Be aware of loud, obnoxious patrons whose attitudes are affected to great extent by alcohol. Unless they pose an immediate threat to your client, merely advise the management or one of the establishment's many "public relations" personnel that you anticipate a potential problem.

AMUSEMENT PARKS

Get ready for some wild times when you work with a client who likes amusement parks and special rides. I worked with one principal who enjoyed all the water rides, and another who could not resist the roller-coaster-type thrills. When you are in a park, you ride when the client rides unless instructed otherwise. (Fortunately for me, I was the team leader on the latter detail and was able to assign thrill-seekers to the roller coasters.)

Amusement parks are usually low-profile details. Unless you are protecting a major celebrity, there will be little, if any, attention drawn to your client. In fact, unless celebrities are of such magnitude that they can only hope not to be recognized, few people are likely to bother even them. In such a situation, make sure you have an adequate detail to be able to escort your principal immediately to an escape route or safe area (that you know of because of your advance and your contacts with park security).

On the other hand, you should know how things are done when everyone is expecting to see a star and will be able to walk and talk with them. I was the team leader for a major detail that involved about a hundred celebrities. One major international entertainer rented an amusement park in honor of his friends, two huge

Hollywood celebrities, and invited stars from everywhere. The host and guests of honor were brought in by helicopter, and everyone else arrived in limousines.

The way such an ordeal takes place is that the park is open to the public until a certain time (this day it was four o'clock in the afternoon). Then only those on the guest list are allowed in a special entrance. A section of the park is set aside for their private party, but the entire park is open for their enjoyment. Another privilege is that when guests select a particular ride, they are escorted with their detail up the exit and allowed preferred seats. The general public then joins for the ride.

This is the type of detail where you must maintain above-average mental alertness. It cannot be compared to a crowd-control job because everyone is allowed to mingle with the stars. The regular, paying visitors are informed that the party is a private affair and that there will be no autograph or photo sessions on the agenda (of course, many celebrities will stop and greet the public).

The private party assignment is the same as that for any private gathering. The public has no access to this area, which has been reserved specifically for the tributes to the guests of honor and dinner. As for dinner, the team leader arranges for the detail to dine after all principals and guests have been served. This is generally done shift-style so that protection is always being provided.

Whenever you plan to visit a park or attend a major event, always notify the appropriate security. These people can prove to be very helpful should you need any assistance.

MOVIE SETS

Whether you are on an actual movie set or out on location filming a movie, the protection varies only slightly. On a set, perimeter security will not allow the public onto the lot, whereas on location, the filming takes place in the public area. On location, your own perimeter security must keep the public at a distance, while the inner circle provides the immediate security for the star.

A filming assignment can become very boring. After the novelty of how a movie is made wears off, the long hours and repetition of retakes set in. However, you have got to stay completely alert for the times when your principal moves from the set to his private areas and back. But bear in mind that the experience you gain and the contacts you make will be invaluable for the remainder of your career.

GENERAL ASSIGNMENTS

Any variation in executive protection details will occur mainly when you are in settings that do not require specific positioned assignments such as a hallway, restaurant, or other previously discussed areas. In such cases, with few exceptions, your position during travel will be dictated by the mode of transportation, such as an airliner or a vessel at sea. Now the principal can request that you be positioned anywhere (e.g., next to him on a flight, to the front or rear of a yacht) to join in the activities or at a location where your duties will be obvious to the guests of associates. Here are some guidelines for other notable details:

   • *Corporate jets*: Try to be the last one on and the first off. In flight, you will know immediately if there are any areas you should avoid.
   • *Commercial airlines*: Get seats directly behind or behind and to the side of your client.
   • *Yachts*: When there are guests aboard, you will assume the most advantageous position without crowding anyone or appearing to be part of the party. If the principal decides to participate in water sports, you can observe

while on the yacht for the most part. If he water skis, you should be in the boat pulling him, and if he's using a jet ski, you should be on one at a wide distance, ready to react immediately.

• *Private parties*: Most are low profile, so blend in. Drink only "executive cocktails" (no alcohol), socialize, and keep an eye on your principal without crowding him. How you are introduced will determine your conversations with others. Many times you are a "cousin," "family friend," "business associate," or any other fictitious title that might be chosen when "security" would distract guests and detract from the party atmosphere.

• *Private homes, estates, and palaces*: The key to remember here is, do not enter unless you are invited. Upon arrival, many agents feel the need to escort the principal into the principal residence. The proper procedure is to arrive on the property, observe the principal enter, and go to the area designated as a waiting room for the security agents. As the clients appear outside the home or prepare to leave, you will be advised by radio contact with others.

• *Corporate offices*: Your position will depend on the threat level and length of employment. On a low-threat assignment that is part of long-term employment, you will escort the principal to and from his or her business circles. On a medium- to high-threat-level detail, you may be introduced as an associate and become part of the general business activities. In such a case, brief yourself on company business enough to play the assigned role.

The Detail

As far as executive protection policies and strategies are concerned, there is little variation, regardless of the principal or the location. My experience has allowed me to work with agents in many countries, and it is always a pleasure to see that the professionals do it the same everywhere.

Expect the Unexpected

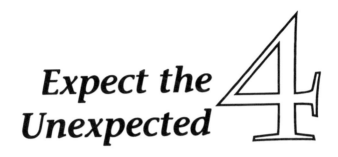

The primary function of a bodyguard is to prevent an attack or problem from occurring. The secondary purpose is to handle a situation if it does occur. So your job is prevention. The more you plan, the more you anticipate, the more experienced you become, the lower the probability of problems.

Anticipating problem situations involves a never-ending mental exercise while you are working a detail. It may be long-term, such as an advance survey for a proposed trip, or short-term for on-the-spot situations. Always be aware of your surroundings and the potential problems. Then, mentally handle them before they occur. On one trip, I was in London working with a Saudi prince. We came out of a restaurant, and he stopped to say something to the owner. This resulted in the entourage blocking the street with three cars and his blocking the sidewalk. I saw two rough-looking skinheads coming toward the group, and they had to pass me. To avoid any possible problems by asking them to hold up or go around, I positioned myself against the building and prepared for my next move. Upon their arrival within 2 feet of me, I looked up at the lights and architecture, stepped directly in front of them, and said, "Excuse me, I wasn't paying attention—your city is so beautiful!" Both stated something unpleasant and stepped into the street, walking around the group! Mission accomplished; no problems.

The better you become at anticipating problems, the less likely they are to occur. To protect your client against the possibility of attacks of any type, or even embarrassing situations, you must be prepared in every way. Prevention by anticipation requires an acute knowledge of your client—his plans, routes, and habits.

The most important thing to avoid in preparing your plan of protection is routine. A client who performs an activity in a routine manner is a likely candidate for any type of attacker. There is a common saying in this business that serves to put everyone on guard: "A terrorist only has to be lucky once; we have to be lucky all the time."

A person planning an attack will watch his target for a period of time. A bodyguard's job is to look at the obvious surroundings while being aware of the inconspicuous at all times. In other words, *think like an attacker*—be it a mere fan wanting to touch your client, a stalker fantasizing, or a terrorist planning a kidnapping.

Many of the most professional protectors play a mental game of "What would I do if . . ." or "How could I cause . . ." and then guard against the vulnerable area that would result in successfully answering one of the questions. The entire purpose of an advance detail is preparing for potential problems, and to do so, you must play this game all the time. Suppose, for instance, that you are driving north on a boulevard you know your principal will be traveling. You note every potential point an attacker could come from, and then—very importantly—drive the same route south! The reason for checking the route both ways is to anticipate problems by thinking like an attacker and observing (1) the client's route while considering all vulnerable areas and (2) the route from the attacker's viewpoint. Traveling in the opposite direction allows you to see the route from the attacker's viewpoint.

As you are conducting an advance, you will also be making note of escape routes in case there is a problem. Always have a primary and secondary plan, both for the general route and the escape routes. And make yourself a promise that you will never fall into the routine trap by using some other person's prior advance or one of your old ones; revisit and rework your plan every time.

Regardless of the assigned position in a detail, you are responsible for anticipating problems. Appropriate advice for an executive protection specialist to keep in mind is "if you fail to plan, plan to fail."

Begin an advance security checklist by obtaining your client's travel itinerary (usually from the secretary). Make sure you have everything to make the client's trip comfortable and successful. Your advance should include all routes, hotels, preferred restaurants, necessary medical needs, and emergency facilities.

The primary purpose of conducting an advance is to anticipate any problems and be prepared to counter them. As you become more familiar with your client, you will also include a list of the items he enjoys that contribute to a comfortable life-style, e.g., his newspaper preferences, massage services, special concerts, etc. Following are some basic forms that you may revise to meet the needs of your client, as well as samples of advance reports.

EXECUTIVE PROTECTION

Advance Report
(Overview)

Date of arrival: _____

Principal: _____

Arrival site: _____

Departure site: _____

Date of arrival/time: _____

Expected departure: _____

Hotel: _____

Address: _____

Phone: _____

Room(s): _____

Transportation by: _____

Routes from arrival to hotel: _____

Maps attached: _____

Estimated time of travel: _____

Police department: _____

Phone: _____

Emergency response time: _____

Fire department/ambulance: _____

Phone: _____

Emergency response time: _____

Medical problems: _____

Prescribed medications: _____

Glasses: _____

24-hr. optometrist: _____

Phone: _____

Doctor: _____

Phone: _____

Purpose of visit: _____

Major concerns: _____

Survey conducted by: _____

Date: _____

Expect the Unexpected

Advance Report (Sample)
(Overview)

Date of arrival: June 1, 1991
Principal: William Arnett
Arrival site: Portland International
Departure site: Same
Date of arrival/time: June 3, 1991/4:45 P.M.
Expected departure: June 10, 1991
Hotel: Hilton Towers
Address: 600 South Street, Portland
Phone: (503) 621-5000
Room(s): Presidential Suite

Transportation by: ABC Limousines
Routes from arrival to hotel: I-205 South to I-84 West
      to City Center, exit to South Street
Maps attached: Yes—route highlighted in blue
Estimated time of travel: 20 minutes

Police department: Portland—South Station
Phone: (503) 286-4100
Emergency response time: Approx. 5 min.
Fire department/ambulance: Portland—South Station
Phone: (503) 286-2200
Emergency response time: Approx. 7 min.
Medical problems: High blood pressure
Prescribed medications: Prinivil, Atenolol
Glasses: Bifocals
24-hour optometrist: Jim Bryan
Phone: (503) 552-1212
Doctor: Gary Roberts, M.D.
Phone: (503) 656-4221
Purpose of visit: Recreation
Major concerns: Private golf courses, spas, beach facilities
Survey conducted by: Roy Bates
Date: May 30, 1991

EXECUTIVE PROTECTION

Routing Report

Arrival date: _____

Arrival time: _____

Site of arrival: _____

Destination: _____

Distance: _____

Primary route: _____

Estimated time: _____

Secondary route: _____

Estimated time: _____

Hospitals and medical facilities en route: _____

Variations day/night concerns: _____

Special areas: _____

Potential hazards: _____

Arrival time at destination: _____

Contact at destination: _____

Phone: _____

Hotel: _____ Room: _____

Advance check-in: _____

Address: _____

Phone: _____

Incidents: _____

Reports attached: _____

Survey conducted by: _____

Date: _____

Routing Report (Sample)

Arrival date: May 5, 1992
Arrival tme: 6:00 P.M.
Site of arrival: Garrett Aviation
Destination: Los Angeles Sheraton
Distance: 16 miles
Primary route: I-405 North to I-10, east to I-110 North,
    Exit Broadway to 6th Street—on right
Estimated time: 25 min.
Secondary route: Sepulveda Blvd. north to Wilshire Blvd.,
    east to 6th Street—on right
Estimated time: 40 min.
Hospitals and medical facilities en route:
    Primary Route: LA General Hospital—
    I-10 to Vermont Exit, one mile north
    Secondary Route: Kaiser Hospital—
    on Wilshire at Sepulveda
Variations day/night concerns:
    Road construction on Secondary Route
    between 10th & 12th Streets via Wilshire
Special areas: Interchange of I-10 and I-11,
    busiest point of all freeways
Potential hazards: LaBrea Tar Pits (secondary route),
    site of many demonstrations
Arrival time at destination: 6:45 P.M.
Contact at destination: Robert Davis, Associate
Phone: (213) 485-2000
Hotel: Los Angeles Sheraton   **Room:** 800
Advance check-in: Yes
Address: 1200 West Sixth Street **Phone:** (213) 485-2000
Incidents: None
Reports attached: Maps of city—
    Primary route in yellow, secondary route in blue
Survey conducted by: Tammy Dennis
Date: May 4, 1992

EXECUTIVE PROTECTION

Restaurant Advance

Date: _____

Name: _____
Location: _____
Phone: _____

General cuisine: _____
_____
_____

Manager: _____
Business card: _____
Maitre d': _____

Reservations: _____
Table/room: _____
Servers: _____
Location: _____

Dress code: _____

Arrangements with: _____

Bill to be paid by: _____

Directions: _____
_____

Advance by: _____
_____
_____

Expect the Unexpected

Restaurant Advance (Sample)

Date: May 10, 1993

Name: Golden Dragon
Location: 1080 Bundy Drive, Beverly Hills
Phone: 310-452-1212

General cuisine: Chinese

Manager: Mr. Roy Wong
Business Card: Yes
Maitre d': Mr. Bill Lee

Reservations: May 11, 8:30 P.M.
Table/room: Eagle Room (private)
Servers: Ted & Sue
Location: Entrance—left to rear—secluded—no windows

Dress code: Upscale casual

Arrangements with: Manager—Mr. Wong

Bill to be paid by: Dennis—Team Leader

Directions: from hotel—Wilshire exit, left turn to
White Avenue, White Avenue to Bundy Drive—
on right, SW corner

Advance by: Lou Smith

Hotel Advance
(Low Profile)

Hotel: _____

Location: _____

Address: _____

Phone: _____

Principal's room: _____

Location: _____

Routes: _____

Emergency exits: _____

Amenities: _____

Television: _____

Channels: _____

Reception: _____

Radio: _____

AM/FM: _____

Channels: _____

Reception: _____

Alarms: _____

Wake up: _____

Telephone: _____

Dialing codes—local—long distance—room to room:

_____

_____

Security: _____

Door type: _____

Dead bolt: _____

Peep hole: _____

Smoke detectors: _____

In room safe: _____

Hotel Advance (Cont'd)

Emergency services: ————————————————

Fire—Police—Paramedics:——————————————
Phone numbers:————————————————
Locations:————————————————
Response time:————————————————

Hospitals: ————————————————
Phone numbers: ————————————————
Locations: ————————————————

Pharmacy:————————————————
Phone numbers:————————————————
Locations:————————————————
Hours of operation: ————————————————

In-house medical facilities/services: ——————————
Routes to medical facilities—direct and alternate:——————
————————————————

Guest facilities: ————————————————

Room service—hours—menu—bar:——————————

Housekeeping—hours—evening service: ——————
————————————————

Laundry—hours—return time:————————————

Gift shop—hours—location—general items: ——————
————————————————

Recreation—gym—pool, etc.:————————————
Locations: ————————————————
Hours:————————————————

Hotel Advance (Cont'd)

Restaurants/Nightclubs:

Name:_____
Location:_____
Hours:_____
Type of service/music/crowds:_____
Menu:_____
Availability: _____

Hotel personnel:

Manager/Assistant Manager:_____
Director of Security:_____
Food and Beverage Manager:_____
Executive Housekeeper:_____
Bell Captain: _____
Maintenance Director:_____
Recreation Facilities Manager:_____

Conclusion:

Statement of hotel's rating:_____
Nearby activities—distances:_____
Available meeting facilities:_____
General safety of area: _____
Overall quality of service:_____

Attach maps, brochures, and all available pertinent publications.

Hotel Advance (Sample)
(Low Profile)

Hotel: The Four Seasons Hotel
Location: 1800 Star Avenue
Los Angeles, CA 90210
(310) 555-1212

Entrance is on circular, cobblestone drive way off Santa Monica Blvd. Doors lead directly to main lobby. Elevators are on right. (Transportation routes from airport attached with city map.)

Principal's room: Presidential Suite. Tenth floor. Exit elevators, left to northeast corner—end of hallway on right. Secluded area from elevators, machines, and traffic. Emergency exit adjacent to suite—25 feet.

Amenities: King-size bed—firm mattress and pillows. Private terrace—no access from exterior. Wet bar—stocked with food and liquor. Oversized washroom—dual sinks and vanity mirrors.

Television: Large 50″ color screen in general area, 26″ color in bedroom. Two small 8″ black and whites in bathroom. All units receive 32 channels. Reception—excellent.

Radio: AM-FM capabilities wired throughout suite.
Reception: Crystal clear—40 stations. Radio near bed has wake-up alarm/music service.
Telephone: Direct dialing available—Long distance, 8 + number; local, 9 + number; room-to-room 7 + room number. Hotel operator available 24 hours.

Security: Double doors are solid oak, 2" thick. Doors are secured with a general lock and deadbolt and have a peephole and intercom service. There is a three-chime doorbell. Every room in the suite has a smoke alarm. The in-room safe may be programmed with a personal code.

Emergency services:

Police: Los Angeles Police Department   525-1202
West Los Angeles Division
Response time: Approx. 7 min.

Fire: Los Angeles Fire Department   525-1010
Station 57
Response time: Approx. 5 min.
Paramedics operate with fire dept.

Hospital: St. John's Hospital   821-1600
Eight blocks from hotel
Response time: Under 5 min.

Pharmacy: Four Seasons Pharmacy
Across street from hotel on northwest corner
24-hour service—hotel will fill prescriptions

In house: The hotel provides a 24-hour on-call physician for minor medical needs.

Route to St. John's hospital: End of driveway, turn right onto Olympic—eight blocks, hospital emergency room is on right (large red entrance sign).

Alternate Route: Exit hotel on east side, near Barney's Pub. Left turn to Santa Monica Blvd., right turn to White Ave., right turn to Olympic Blvd., right turn—emergency room on left.

Guest facilities:

Room service is available 24 hours with complete menu. Bar service is available until 2:00 A.M. Housekeeping service is available from 7:00 A.M. to 10:00 P.M. Laundry and dry cleaning service are available from 6:00 A.M. to 8:00 P.M. Laundry will be returned within three hours; dry cleaning in four hours or next day if applicable. Special requests are available.

The gift shop is on the ground floor next to Dom Pierre's. The hours are 6:00 A.M. to 10:00 P.M. Most gift shop items are available through room service 24 hours a day.

The recreation area includes a heated pool, wet and dry sauna, complete gym, and barber and beauty shop services. This is the "Pamper & Play" area located on the ground floor in the southwest corner. The hours are 6:00 A.M. to 10:00 P.M., with the exception of the barber and beauty shops—8:00 A.M. to 6:00 P.M., with appointments available before, during, and after hours.

Restaurants/Nightclubs:

Coffee Elegant is located on the main floor. Provides all meals in a casual setting. Open 24 hours.

Surf & Turf is located on the ground floor. Serves late lunch and dinner. Menu is seafood and steaks. Dress is casual. Hours: 4:00 P.M. to midnight.

Dom Pierre's is located on the ground floor, left of the gift shop. The cuisine is French. Jackets are required. Reservations are suggested. Hours: 6:00 P.M. to 1:00 A.M.

Barney's Pub is an upscale bar catering to after-work clientele from the nearby areas. It is located on the first floor, directly to the rear of the front desk. This is the lobby lounge. Service is available from 11:00 A.M. to 2:00 A.M.

Diamonds & Pearls is the hotel's nightclub. It is located on the top floor of the hotel, providing a complete view of the city. Live music on Thursdays, Fridays, and Saturdays. Disco other days. Upscale, casual attire. No cover charge for hotel guests. Hours: 7:00 P.M. to 2:00 A.M.

Hotel personnel:

	Extension
Manager: Thelma Baker	211
Assistant Manager: Richard Day	212
Director of Security: Victor Roberts	300
Food & Beverage Manager: Penny Wright	200
Executive Housekeeper: Barbara Martin	101
Maintenance Director: Brian Casey	125
Rec. Facilities Manager: Joanne Hill	150

Conclusion:

The Four Seasons Hotel is a five-star and four-diamond facility. It is situated within walking distance to all of the area's finest restaurants and entertainment facilities. There are several rooms and a wide variety of floor space for business meetings. The crime rate is very low in this area and nearly nonexistent for the hotel. The overall quality of service of the hotel is excellent.

City maps, hotel brochures, and entertainment guides are attached.

High-Profile Assignments 5

Primarily throughout this book I have discussed the operations of low-profile details. The majority of my writing has been devoted to these assignments, because it is a fact that more than 90 percent of details are low-profile. I could almost guarantee that your initial positions in any detail will be on the low side. I am not referring to a fixed post, where mere presence is used as a deterrence (a uniformed security guard could perform that function). I am talking about the responsibilities for a moving detail. The high-profile detail, however, has its place for clients who are not corporate executives or very rich, for whom "blending in" is a necessity. The high-profile assignment is as close as you can get to the stereotypical image of a "bodyguard." In this situation, the sunglasses, earpieces, body armor, and weapons are considered acceptable, if de rigeur. These serve as an announcement to a potential attacker, and everyone else, that the client is protected. When executive protection specialists look the part, a strong signal is sent that they are professionals and prepared for action.

When you are sending a strong warning merely by

your appearance, you must be mentally alert at all times. It has often been said that a bodyguard must be paranoid all the time and develop an attitude that no one is to be trusted. This is especially true on a high-profile detail.

A high-profile detail is generally called for when there have been attempts to harm the client, threats to the client have been made and verified as viable, or the principal's status alone subjects him or her to potential harm.

In every situation, you must be ready to react, but this is particularly crucial in a high-profile assignment, where the action is instantaneous. Your skills must be so finely tuned that your split-second reaction is automatic. There is no room for error or second-guessing. You must protect the client at all costs. You must be willing to shield your principal from all harm, even if doing so means risking your own life.

Several years ago, a well-recognized celebrity and his wife were at the front desk of a hotel in another country when someone threw a smoke bomb into the lobby. This star's two bodyguards apparently dove for cover as he walked away from all the attention. When I interviewed with the celebrity, one of the questions I had to answer was how I would have reacted under such circumstances. Without hesitating (very important with interview questions that involve scenarios), I answered that my immediate response would have been to shield the star with my body, with my back to the bomb, and rush him to a safe area. When questioned about the protection of the wife, I stated a fact: my primary responsibility would be to protect the client; even if there was no one assigned to her, I would still react the same and hope she made it to safety. I was offered the position and served as the team leader for the actor for several years.

I mentioned earlier that it is good practice to play mind games with yourself and other team members during slow times. The "what if this happens?" game will help to educate you because it continually gives you new ideas while keeping you and the team mentally alert. I used to present a scenario to police officers who thought their law enforcement experience was enough to get them into the profession but lacked all knowledge of executive protection procedures. I asked them what their immediate reaction would be if they were working a two-man detail—one to the front and the other to the rear of the principal—and the front agent was attacked by two large men from a crowd. Invariably, their answers centered around helping their partner. They thought like police officers, as they had been trained. They always looked at me in disbelief when I told them the proper procedure would be to turn your principal in the opposite direction of the fight, shield him with your body, and get him out of there as fast as possible. If your partner survives, he will catch up with you later. Your only concern is the safety of the client. Any other action would leave the principal vulnerable.

Personal protection specialists know they must be in very close proximity to the person they are protecting, in case it becomes necessary to ward off any attack or shield the client from an attack by stepping in front of him or her while another team member removes the principal to a safe area. Generally, each agent's responsibility is outlined in his or her game plan and must be interchangeable with other agents' responsibilities. How an individual agent reacts depends upon the direction from which the attack originates.

I have been asked repeatedly by friends and relatives after they found out whom I had been protecting, "Why would anyone want to hurt him, or her, or children?" What many people, including inexperienced agents, fail to realize is that "hurting" someone is generally the least of the attacker's intentions. Their goal is usually to kidnap your client. Ransom money from kidnappings is a major source of revenue for terrorists around the world, and many opportunists try to cash in when they see an easy target.

This is a prime example of why a protection specialist must not only have a working knowledge of terrorism but also think like the terrorist, or common criminal, and play the "what if" mind games.

The study of terrorism should not focus exclusively on the Middle East situation, the Irish Republic Army, the Japanese Red Army, or any other particular group or situation. It must center on the overall groups that are well known for their strong feelings of animosity for each other. You must be armed with sufficient knowledge to know which groups, as well as individuals, to protect your client from. This means a practical understanding of any potential animosity focused on your client because of race, religion, skin color, and political or moral beliefs, among many other reasons. (Review the section relating to the study of terrorism in "Bodyguards.")

A word about firearms: in the world of protecting others, they should be used as a last resort. Even the displaying of weapons should be understood as an act of force undertaken only if necessary. Most actions on a detail can be rationalized and corrected if required. However, in the use of weapons there is a very thin line between right and wrong.

Before you label me an antigun fanatic, let me express the importance of being familiar with several guns. That is, select the weapons you would be comfortable using on the various details, practice with them until you know everything about them, become an expert at firing each gun, and become relaxed about carrying one concealed. Then, don't be afraid to use it when such use is absolutely necessary.

As you gain experience, you will understand what makes a professional. Being prepared does not mean having to use everything available, and your knowledge will give you the necessary split-second ability to make the correct decision. When you reach the professional level, others will notice, and you will be called upon more often to be part of the teams assigned to high-profile details.

The Command Post

6

The Command Post (CP) is the center of every operation. It is the focal point of all team members. The detail begins and ends here. Communication among the detail members through the CP is an absolute necessity. I have always said that if there is going to be problem it will be because of a breakdown in communication.

The CP agent is the busiest person on any detail. He is responsible for knowing the location of every agent, principal, and driver at all times. He or she must coordinate all activities, respond to every request, and keep accurate records in order to refer to current and past events. Even incidents and contacts made during a client's previous visits must be readily available. Clients will occasionally repeat those activities they enjoy. (Be thankful for computers.)

The CP can be hectic at times, especially during major and critical events. The CP agent must have an extraordinary level of self-control and patience. Because everything is directed through him, he must also be an excellent public relations person; the wrong response could cause the client and the team unnecessary problems.

The following are examples of some records and forms the CP must keep for the client. Because itineraries change so often, the forms should be provided to the team on a daily basis. Every agent should be cognizant of the confidentiality of these lists and reports.

SECURITY SPECIAL ORDERS

Mobile Units

Drivers
- Drivers are to remain with their vehicles at all times.
- Security drivers will carry a two-way radio at all times.
- Drivers of principals will carry a two-way radio and cellular telephone at all times.
- During waiting periods at the house, drivers will remain in designated driver's room and stand by to be called.
- Dress code for drivers requires neat, conservative attire.
- Drivers will remain on duty until released by the CP.

(Note: Those who are not principal drivers are chase car drivers.)

Security Mobile Team
- Each team will keep the CP advised of its principal's location at all times.
- Each team will carry a cellular phone, and each team member will carry a two-way radio.
- During waiting periods at the house, agents will remain in the designated room, behind the CP, until called.
- Agents will remain on duty until the CP releases their team.
- Dress code for each agent will depend upon expected activity during that day's assignment.

House
- All gates will be kept closed at all times.
- No vehicles are to be admitted into any gate unless authorized by the CP or other authority.
- All visitors are to check in and receive authorization from agent at main gate.
- Visitors will be escorted by roving agent to and from their destinations.

Fixed Positions
- Agents will not leave their posts unless relieved. Relief for necessary breaks will be coordinated through the CP.
- Agents at gates will keep gates closed when not admitting or exiting vehicle/persons.
- A written log will be maintained by the agent at the main gate. The entries will include time in/out, organization, purpose of visit, person to be visited, and expected length of visit.
- No visitors are to be admitted unless agent is satisfied that the visitor should be admitted. All questionable visits should be cleared by the CP.
- Dress of agents at gate should be neat and conservative, creating a well-groomed appearance.

Command Post
- CP will be the center of all security activity.
- CP will be manned 24 hours per day.
- CP will be kept advised of locations of principals at all times.
- CP will promptly report any problems or important security matters to an appropriate supervisor or authority.
- CP will immediately respond to any emergency and keep all emergency phone numbers on display.

Personnel List
January 10, 1994

Principals		Rooms
#1	Mr. Robert Smith	Presidential Suite
#2	Mrs. Victoria Smith	Presidential Suite
#3	Ms. Esther Smith	Room 1601
#4	Ms. Allison Smith	Room 1601
#5	Mr. Timothy Smith	Room 1602

Public Relations Officer

Mr. Tom Boeing	Room 1610

Private Secretary

Ms. Wendy Lee	Room 1612

Personal Nurse

Ms. JoAnn Jenkins	Room 1603

Protection Detail

Mr. Dennis Sergeant, Team Leader
Room 1604

Mr. Ian Carston
Room 1607

Mr. Austin John
Room 1607

Ms. Emily Kidd
Room 1608

Ms. Kathy Kaiser
Room 1608

Ms. Pamela Fisher
Room 1609

Ms. Stacey Faye
Room 1609

Mr. Gerry Clayton
Room 1614

EXECUTIVE PROTECTION

Security Phone Numbers

Name	Cellular	Pager	
Brown	485-2212	679-2134	Ext. 7205
Smith	485-2212	679-2135	Ext. 7205
Davis	485-2213	679-2136	Ext. 7206
Peters	485-2213	679-2137	Ext. 7206
Dennis	485-2214	679-2138	Ext. 7207
Boyles	485-2214	679-2139	Ext. 7207
Thompson	485-2215	679-2140	Ext. 7208
Roberts	485-2215	679-2141	Ext. 7208

Hotel: 734-5000
Security: Ext. 5201
Airport Police: 879-6231
City Police: 737-2121
Emergency: 911
Fire Department: 737-4321
Emergency: 911
Command Post: 734-5678

The Command Post

Activities

Principal #1
June 15, 1994

Time	Activity
11:00	Left hotel—en route to Wilshire Mall
11:08	Arrived Wilshire Mall
11:14	Entered Nordstrom Department Store
12:02	Left Nordstrom
12:15	Entered Orange's Restaurant
13:20	Left restaurant
13:30	Entered Macy's Department Store
13:35	Left Macy's
13:40	Movies—United Artist
15:10	Exited theater—en route to hotel
15:20	Arrived hotel—Presidential Suite
18:05	Left hotel—en route to cheesecake factory
19:15	Left restaurant—en route to Main St., cousin's house
19:40	Arrived cousin's house
21:20	Left house—en route to beach
21:50	Arrived S.M. Beach
22:30	Left beach for hotel
23:00	Arrived hotel—Presidential Suite. Secured for evening.

Driver: Bob   **Team #1**
Pagers: Victor 986-5602   **Phone:** 371-5209
            Sam 986-5600   **Phone:** 371-6565

Compensation 7

Any discussion of compensation in the protection field must always include an in-depth explanation of the schedules you can expect to work, depending upon your client. An assignment with a particular principal will generally give an experienced agent an indication of how many hours are going to be included for the rate of compensation for the day, week, or month. Very seldom will a company contract with a client on an hourly basis. However, short- term assignments, such as providing protection from an airport to a final destination, may be contracted on an hourly basis. A transportation detail would require only a few hours. Hourly rates should generally be paid only for assignments comprising a minimum number of hours.

A bodyguard can typically expect an assignment to require at least 12 hours per day. This is generally the stated shift for guarding a fixed post, such as a hallway. The hours of other positions can vary with one's imagination. A few scenarios follow, but remember, you are there for the convenience of the client, and the conduct of the clients is not necessarily based on concern for your hours.

Corporate Executives. This type of principal offers the best chance for a fairly predictable schedule. Plan to be ready for breakfast about an hour or two before a regular business day begins. The level of threat will determine whether you will be in a fixed location for the day or work on an on-call basis. After-work activities will include going out for dinner, especially on out-of-town trips, and possibly to a show or nightclub. Expect the evening to end late and start early again the next day.

Celebrities. There are two basic schedules you can expect when working with celebrities, and both require your presence near the star. The first type of assignment is easier, but more demanding in terms of remaining alert in the face of boredom. It involves being with the client while he or she is working, whether making a movie, rehearsing for a concert, or filming in a television studio. Generally there is security in every area, so your only concern is your principal's every move. I recall one incident that occurred when a star, while filming a scene, observed two bodyguards talking. The star silently signaled the director, left the set, hid behind some curtains, and monitored the reaction of the bodyguards and the time that passed before they found him. Fortunately, he had a good sense of humor and enjoyed practical jokes, but the point was well made with regard to alertness.

The second type of schedule is just as demanding in terms of mental awareness but is seldom boring. It involves moving with the celebrity and watching the crowds, fans, and everyone in general. A shift such as this could include an early morning workout, visitations all day, evening get-togethers or parties, late night dinners and clubs, and the trip back home. Basically, it could consist of any number of hours.

Royalty. Now for the most interesting clients. I will address primarily Middle Eastern royal families, because the majority of my experience involved traveling with and protecting these clients. When money is not an object, their regular discussions involve where and when to travel. Here we are not talking about their annual two-week vacation, but their one-month to three-month trips.

The hours involved on an assignment with royalty will depend mainly on the age of the principal. Children of younger ages will basically involve about six to eight hours; teenagers, 10 to 14; young adults, especially young princes—Allah only knows! Vacation time is the time for young princes to see, do, and have almost everything they want, and believe me, sleep is not high on their agendas. I have worked details where the agents had to revolve in shifts to maintain the hours the client kept. When you travel as part of the entourage, the "average" day is 16-plus hours. Protection of older royalty involves more normal hours; that is, eight to ten per day.

Other Clients: This includes all the incidental clients, the attorney's protectees, the one-time clients, and people who feel the need for protection at parties or special events. The assigned hours are controlled by the level of threat and the customer's need to make certain appointments. This category is the most likely to involve the hourly rate.

Rates of compensation vary in different areas of the United States, as well as other countries. An inexperienced agent can expect wages of $125 to $200 per day, which will most likely include all expenses such as meals, lodging, and transportation. In the event the assignment is local (i.e., no agents need to be brought in from other areas), the rate could be hourly and would not include the benefits except expenses incurred while with the client. The average hourly rate depends on an agent's experience and ranges from $10 to $30. The rates quoted are primarily for services contracted through a company. Therefore, you have only the responsibility for protecting your assignee and yourself with rendering professional service.

When you decide to go solo or start your own team

and contract directly with the client, be careful. Keep in mind that the larger bodyguard companies are experienced in business and aware of not only the many opportunities, but also the many potential pitfalls.

One agent, whom I will refer to as Paul, contacted with a client through several assignments and was called directly by the client for a rather lucrative detail. The request was for a team of six agents to meet the client at a resort that was halfway across the country from the agent's home. Paul, experienced for a couple of years, became the team leader and recruited five of his friends from other details to complete the team.

Paul, planning to conduct a good advance of the area, arrived a day early with his agents and called the client the following morning in anticipation of his arrival later that evening. The public relations officer for the client's corporation advised Paul that due to unexpected business, the principal's arrival would be delayed for three days, which meant the plane would land by Wednesday. A few days later, this officer contacted Paul and informed him that he fully expected they would be arriving by the weekend, saying he would call back with flight plans.

By now, Paul had exhausted his bankroll, and the team members began pooling their funds and cashed in their return airline tickets to survive until the detail began. On Monday, Paul was told that the client had to change his plans, appreciated Paul's efforts, and would call him upon the next trip. The client felt no expenses were due because the trip never occurred. Paul's team returned home after borrowing from friends and relatives. Unlike with a large agency, Paul did not have enough resources to battle the client and suffered the loss.

The moral of Paul's dilemma is until you are ready to play in the big leagues, do not try to deal directly with a client without authorization from the company that is hiring you. Plus, accept the opportunity to gain your experience from a reputable company as long as you can.

I was fortunate to be a pioneer in providing executive protection services on the West Coast after receiving extensive training from the finest trainers on the East Coast. I developed a policy that never failed me throughout many years in this business. Upon receiving an initial request for services from a client who had no track record (through referrals) involving any travel, my response was to ask the following questions: (1) Where could I pick up my round-trip airline tickets? (2) Whose account would cover my hotel? (3) What was the initial period of service requested? I would request the fee in advance for the first period. In the event the client refused my request, I interpreted this as a sign of distrust of me, and therefore there was no contract. I always asked the above questions before they became an issue, because if the client initially requested that I cover my own expenses and invoice the corporation, my refusal or negotiation at that point would reflect a distrust of the client. Again, this policy always proved successful for me. Once a client had established a track record for reliability, I never had a problem advancing my personal funds for expenses relating to requested services.

I want to caution you in another area, and that is know your worth, but be flexible. Be aware of the going price for various services, but be careful not to underprice your services or get into a bidding war for price. On the other hand, know the client's needs, wants, and boundaries, and make the client aware of the professionalism offered by your experience. Many times when you feel you are worth a certain amount, that is not what the client is willing to pay, even though you are the agent he or she wants. You can take the position of "then let the client get someone else." This philosophy is acceptable if you have established a reputation and your experience speaks for itself, but until that time, go with the flow.

One time a client from Los Angeles called for two

agents for a week assignment in Paris. The offered pay was $400 per day, business class travel, with all expenses paid. One agent demanded $1,000 per day because he spoke French. He lost out on the detail. The job was filled immediately, all went well, and everyone was satisfied. A week later the agent with the high demand called to see if the assignment was still available and said that he had had second thoughts and would take it.

Again, know what the market will bear. Do not sacrifice your professionalism when your experience supports your demands, but be willing to work with a client who is sincere. In today's economy, clients do a little shopping for bargains, but few sacrifice professionalism for price.

The bottom line—whether you work for a company or, after sufficient experience and training, market yourself—is that the field of executive protection has yet to reach its peak. As a profession of the future, it offers a wide variety of benefits.

Etiquette, Dining, and Dress 8

Throughout this book, I have stressed the importance of a personal protection specialist's ability to blend in with the corporate and family structures. This chapter deals with the social graces and appearances that enhance them. Your mastery of these areas will be the key to your future in executive protection.

There is a strong correlation between a personal protection specialist and an actor or actress. When you decide to become a true professional in executive protection, you must always know your role. You must continually study your lines, know the character, and be aware of your locations. With each assignment the character/principal changes, and the location/country may be different as well. You must adapt to every change. The more roles you play, the more professional you become. Playing the role of an executive means transforming yourself into an executive and being able to conduct yourself as an executive in every setting.

Think about how often you have heard someone say, "Let's meet for dinner," or, "Let's discuss it over lunch." Business meetings in restaurants have become a way of life in the business world. They give executives an opportunity to evaluate other people in several areas other than the business at hand: their appearance as they enter the room, their manners as they conduct themselves in a relaxed social atmosphere, and their dining habits during the meal. Your failure in any of these areas could result in your being rejected for detail because the client fears that hiring you could eventually lead to an embarrassment.

There are many avenues one can take in pursuit of adequate knowledge in these areas. Every reputable school and course in executive protection includes a thorough discussion of etiquette, dining, and dress, and all recommend follow-up reading material (see "Recommended Reading").

APPROPRIATE DRESS

In 1984, Hart, Schaffner & Marx ran full-page ads that read, "The right suit may not get you on the corporate jet. But the wrong suit could certainly keep you off." That message gets stronger every day as more security agents enter the rapidly expanding field of executive protection. Several years ago I led a team to meet an executive arriving on a private jet. One agent called at the last minute to inform me of an emergency in his family and that he had arranged for a friend with some experience to fill his position. His friend arrived wearing a loud plaid sport coat and brown pants. As the executive departed the plane, he called me aside and asked about the friend. Apologetically, I explained the situation. The executive said, "Have him drive the luggage van to the hotel, and then replace him." Here, the first impression was fatal for this agent's position on the team, but in this business every impression is critical.

It is important not to overdress in a manner that will upstage the principal. This could prove to be not only embarrassing but fatal. Unless informed otherwise, always "dress up" as one would for a corporate business day. It is much easier to "dress down," e.g., take off your tie and coat, roll up your sleeves, and look relaxed, than it is to "dress up" from casual attire. Double-breasted suits are traditionally considered overdressing and generally are inappropriate for a protective detail (they are meant to be buttoned and therefore offer no immediate access to a weapon).

Once when I was on a low-profile detail traveling alone with a principal on a commercial airline, I called a protection company at our destination that had been referred to me. I requested that three agents meet us at the arrival gate and assist me on a four-day detail. Neither group knew the other, and my instructions were that one agent wear a red tie and I would acknowledge him. Upon my arrival with the principal, coming into the airport terminal, we observed three men positioned about thirty feet apart from each other, each wearing sunglasses and ear pieces. The "agent" with the red tie was wearing a double-breasted suit. My principal, obviously as surprised as I was, moved back to me and quietly said, "Don't meet anyone; we'll go to the hotel. You can straighten this out later." Our immediate impression was that these were not experienced agents, and their appearance would draw unwanted attention to us. There is a place for everything, and sunglasses and ear-pieces were inappropriate inside the terminal.

MANNERS AND CUSTOMS

Understanding basic manners (e.g., "Don't speak unless spoken to") and simply being polite will get you through most activities, but not knowing the social graces and customs of other countries and special circles may get you into real trouble.

There are many ways to avoid controversy and divert

attention from yourself and your activities. Keep in mind that what may be sincere and innocent on your part may be construed differently by others, most importantly your client. A perfect example of this is the way you greet others. Make sure all greetings to clients, their friends and associates, and especially their families are strictly generic. Stay away from making remarks like, "You look nice today," or, "My, you smell nice," or, "Wow, you look dressed to kill." Although meant as a compliment, your remark may be construed as flirting, so a "Hello" or "Good morning" is more appropriate.

When you get your first assignments to parties or premieres attended by models and celebrities, do not stare or get involved in lengthy conversations that might be interpreted as flirting. Do not ask for autographs or, after the assignment, become a "name dropper." Executive protection is not a profession for star-struck people, wannabe actors, or gossip columnists. We had one agent who was secretly approaching stars and submitting movie scripts to them. He is no longer in the profession (and, by the way, sold no scripts).

What you do during your off-duty time may be critical. Two major mistakes that occur are drinking in the bars of the hotel the principal is staying in and making excessive room service or restaurant charges. I have witnessed several agents relieved of duty for these actions, even after they were strongly advised against such behavior several times.

Many inexperienced agents feel what they do on their own time is their business and, therefore, they do not see why relaxing in a bar in their hotel should be a problem. The conflict arises when a client, especially a nondrinking client, observes them and is offended. A cardinal rule in every detail is: *Never charge alcohol to the client.* This also applies to the minibars in hotel rooms.

The topic of drinking brings to mind another area of concern. A few years back, I provided security for an international singer who was being followed worldwide by a journalist from a well-known weekly tabloid. The reporter's entire responsibility was to find and write gossip on my client. Now imagine how many people are encouraged and paid by these gossip publications to report activities on celebrities, and keep that firmly in mind when you are off-duty enjoying a drink with a "new friend." Many professionals abstain from all alcohol while assigned to a detail, and this is a good policy for you as well. This way you will always be mentally alert and thinking like a pro.

I have heard excessive meal charges rationalized the same way time after time: "We have to eat, and with their money, why should they care?" True, you have to eat and the client accepts that as part of the budget, but to order steak and lobster every night is excessive, and the client, rightfully, will feel he is being taken advantage of. It is not uncommon for a detail to begin in a first-class hotel and end up in a second-class motel, wondering why they were moved. Listen to the team leader, know your limitations, and remember—you are representing the client in everything you do.

An agent's attitude is extremely important in on- and off-duty performance. In representing the client, bear in mind at all times that he or she is the VIP, not you. Many new agents develop such a superior attitude when their initial assignments put them in five-star hotels, first-class restaurants, and luxury travel, all with VIP treatment, that they treat employees of these establishments and services as their own employees. Always remember that the service you receive is solely because of your principal's status, not yours. In foreign countries, you will avoid the "ugly American" image, and by treating everyone with respect, you will always receive the respect you deserve wherever you go.

Personal hygiene is another critical area. Details often involve long hours, extensive travel, and a variety of climates and conditions. Be prepared for any situation and adequately supplied with items necessary for cleanliness. Avoid strong aftershave or perfume, as these will draw unnecessary attention to you.

Personal conduct with a principal is crucial. Respect for the client never ends. Regardless of the length of employment or terms of agreements, with regard to how to address a client, always remember who is the employer and who is the employee. You are never on the same level. Maintaining this attitude will ensure a greater respect for you while simultaneously establishing job security.

DINING

Your next concern is dining. Bad table manners may not be a reason to dismiss a bodyguard from a detail, but they will be sufficient to cause a reassignment within the detail. Very few team leaders can afford to have offensive table manners, and since they are primarily responsible for the smoothness of a detail, they are generally put in charge of making the assignments. So, if your details seldom, if ever, involve dining with the client, consider a discussion regarding your dining etiquette and table manners.

Customs vary in countries as well as in different social circles, but for the most part, a working knowledge of general manners and procedures will get you by as you gain your personal experience. I will highlight a few examples, but a good rule is when in doubt, follow the actions of others.

When you are attending parties, most likely someone will make a toast. The question is always "What do I do—I am working?" Many responses are, "Toast with the water, since you cannot drink." True, you cannot drink, but be advised that in some circles toasting with water is an insult, as it is considered a blank toast. The proper procedure is raise your glass for the toast in honor to the recipient, touch the wine to your lips, and replace the glass on the table.

If in doubt as to which utensil to use (a formal place setting can be pretty confusing at first), start from the outside and work in as the servings arrive. Certain utensils are used for fish dishes, while others are proper for meals consisting of meat. Glasses can be just as confusing. In a formal setting, there may be four or five glasses. Remember the rule: follow the leader.

During the meal, pace yourself with others. No matter how hungry you are, finishing in half the time of everyone else, and looking around saying, "Boy, was I starved!" is not acceptable. As previously mentioned, when the principal gets up to leave, whether you are at the same table or one nearby, you are finished. On that note, when a principal rises to go to the rest room, unless instructed otherwise, one agent will casually follow. However, this is not the rule for male agents protecting a female client on a low-profile detail. In this situation, chances are you will not be seated at the same table as your client, and rising with her will draw unnecessary attention to her visiting the ladies room. Whether or not she is leaving the restaurant will be indicated by who or what is left at the table.

When your detail involves protecting foreign dignitaries, and especially Middle Eastern royalty, note that they enjoy going out for coffee or tea and will sit for hours. However, after a meal they will seldom sit and visit over coffee or tea. They prefer to pay the check, leave, and go somewhere else. So be prepared to notify the drivers to bring the cars up when you see the check being delivered.

If you are entering the profession with a sincere desire to be a personal protection specialist, then you must understand and accept that it takes time and continuous study. Like any major degree, there are numerous required courses and quite a few electives. Etiquette, dining, and dress are required subjects.

Résumés

Every résumé, regardless of length, can and must be written in a positive manner.

The primary purpose of a résumé is to inform the reader of your positive points and create an interest in you that will open the door to the interview with the client.

If you are in the security field but have yet to break the barrier into executive protection, state the time you have been in the field of security and/or the schools you have attended, and anything related to the area of personal protection or being a bodyguard.

I have advised prospective clients to consider seriously not hiring business with interviewees who, within the first five minutes of the interview, relate that they are off-duty police officers, martial arts experts, or active in body building or weight training. Highlighting these areas suggests to the client that you are relying on weapons or power for their protection. As you become more experienced in professional bodyguard work, you will realize that while these are great attributes for the position, they are not the most important, nor are they even critical, to the profession. Avoid mentioning such skills in a résumé or interview unless absolutely necessary.

I worked with an actor for several years before I ever mentioned my martial arts expertise. I revealed my experience only because the client was seeking lessons for several action shots in his next film.

It is very important to remember not to be a name dropper when you prepare your résumé. Do not mention the clients you have provided protection for, either to impress the prospective client or establish credibility for yourself. Confidentiality is an important aspect of the profession and is expected by everyone.

There will be many interviews in which you will be asked to provide the names of previous clients. My suggestion is to be honest at all times, but begin by relating general categories your past protectees fall into, e.g., entertainers, corporate executives, royal families, etc. If the interviewer asks for the specific names, tell him, but never place the names on a résumé.

I have heard agents respond to such questions with, "That information is confidential; I can't reveal it. I would never give anyone your name either." My advice to you is to avoid playing this game with the client and, again, be honest. This person is seeking the same protection as your previous clients and does not pose a threat to them, so answer the questions.

The field of executive protection, although growing rapidly, comprises a small circle of true professionals. Any abuse of the standards generally spreads like wildfire and could seriously impair future opportunities.

It is strongly recommended that your résumé look professional. Consider having a professional résumé service prepare your résumé. If you do it yourself, make sure it is on quality paper and the print quality is excellent, such as from a laser printer. Never send inferior photostatic copies.

Please note that each time your experience or education changes you should redo your résumé. Believe it when I say that many résumés are submitted with additions that stand out so clearly due to misalignment or different type that it distracts the reader. Such distractions could cost you your foot in the door.

Keep your résumé simple. In other words, it should be vague but cover enough of your experience to cause the reader to want to meet with you. Do not try to reveal everything ahead of time—why, then, would they meet with you before making a decision?

If you are an independent who contracts out to several corporations and executives, a word of caution (based on my costly experience). Write your cover letter to heads of security in such a way that you do not appear to be seeking their jobs! Make it clear that you merely want them to consider hiring you to assist them whenever they are in your area or may need you. Note: You must do this tactfully but professionally, so that you make your point effectively (see sample letter).

Unless a salary history is requested, do not submit one with your résumé. Allow yourself to impress the client in an interview and then be able to discuss and negotiate your compensation.

If you do not have executive protection experience, do not fake it! This will come back to haunt you. Highlight your positive points without exaggerating.

Never assume that police, security, or military experience alone qualifies you as a bodyguard. Most experience in these areas is, in reality, perimeter security; it is not provided directly around the client. There is an enormous difference between being a bodyguard, (i.e., merely protecting bodies) and being a professional protector.

Keep your résumé brief. I advise no more than two pages, without the cover letter. Do not go back too far in your personal history, unless it is directly related to the position you are seeking. State all your relevant fields and all major accomplishments in such fields.

Remember, you are submitting your résumé to a level of society that can afford the luxury of your services and, therefore, expects the best. A poorly written or subquality résumé can eliminate you as a potential candidate the moment it is opened and reviewed. There should be no typographical, spelling, or grammatical errors. Have a professional proofreader or someone with excellent English skills proof your résumé before you send it out. As with your appearance, keep in mind, you only get one opportunity to make a first impression with a résumé.

Finally, along with your résumé it is critical that you prepare and submit a personalized cover letter to the prospective client. Avoid the "generic" cover letter, i.e., "Dear Ladies/Gentlemen" or, "Dear Sir," etc. Take the time to address it directly to the person you wish to meet. The extra preparation time will be worth it, and you may be lucky enough to get the interview. Remember the saying, "Luck is where preparation and opportunity meet!"

SAMPLE LETTER

November 10, 1994

Ultimate Designs, Inc.
Mr. Anthony Kipp
Director of Security
2222 Avenue of the Stars
Century City, CA 90290

Dear Mr. Kipp:

The purpose of this letter is to inform you of my qualifications in the field of executive protection and to offer my services when you visit the Los Angeles area.

Please be advised that I am not seeking employment on a full-time basis, as I am very active with several clients at present. I am merely seeking short-term assignments.

As Ultimate Designs, Inc. is highly respected in the clothing industry, I would be greatly complimented if you would review my enclosed résumé and allow me an opportunity to meet with you or phone you to discuss this offer in more detail.

Thank you for your consideration of my services.

Very truly yours,

Michelle Washington

Afterword

It is now time for the "wheels up" party. The detail is over, it was successful, and it is time to celebrate. Generally, on a larger, lengthy assignment, after escorting the principals to their plane, you get together with the team, swap "war" stories, and prepare to leave for your next assignment.

We have had our detail, and now let us briefly review what it takes to get into the field of executive protection and become a successful personal protection specialist.

I remember being approached by an investigator when I was a police officer working off-duty security jobs in the early eighties. He said, "You know, if you really want to have some fun, see the country, and get much better pay while building a future, you should get into executive protection."

"What's executive protection?" I asked.

The investigator replied, "It's a more professional way of being a bodyguard."

I was interested and began researching the field. I read articles in security magazines, heard about several schools, and made arrangements to attend one.

I could say the rest is history, but I want to emphasize the training and groundwork needed to become an active professional in the business. I continued to read as many publications as I could get my hands on, studied the profession in depth, and attended five schools over the years.

I have been asked many times why I continued to go to the schools after having been in the business on numerous details and having already traveled the world. My response has always been the same: if I can find one new idea or method that will add to my knowledge and help me in my profession, then I will keep attending the schools and reading the books. You never stop learning, and you can always improve.

This attitude and approach have helped me gain a lot of experience in a short period of time, and you can do the same.

If you are still interested in this exciting profession, and again, this is the time to join in, then take the following steps to becoming a pro:

- Read as much as possible about the business, so there will be no doubt about your total commitment.
- Select a reputable school and make plans to attend as soon as you can.
- Prepare a résumé, highlighting all related experience and the courses attended.
- Select the companies in your area for local work, and the major organizations for assignments involving travel. Send your résumé and a cover letter to all of them.
- Keep an open mind and absorb information from everyone else's experiences as well as your own.
- Pick a buddy—either a friend, a classmate from your executive protection school, or an agent from an initial assignment (whose experiences and goals are similar to yours) and agree to keep in touch and encourage each other in the pursuit of excellence.

Afterword

As you can see, you can make it in the executive protection field from any background. The fact that I was a police officer had nothing to do with my success in the field. My contacts came from the schools I attended, the people I met along the way, and the encouragement I received.

So, with a positive attitude and a sincere desire to succeed, you should encounter only a minimal number of problems as you begin. Before long, you will have your own experiences. Then it will be your turn to help the next new agent.

Appendix A

Training Facilities

Executive Protection Institute
Richard W. Kobetz & Associates, Ltd.
Arcadia Manor
Route 2, Box 3645
Berryville, VA 22611

Vance International
Chuck Vance
10467 White Granite Drive, Suite 210
Oakton, VA 22124

Scotti International
Anthony J. Scotti
11 Riverside Avenue, Suite 15
Medford, MA 02155

Executive Security International
Bob Duggan
2101 Emma Road
Basalt, CO 81621

Appendix B

Glossary

Every profession has its own terminology, and executive protection is no exception. Basically, our language is supported by terms gathered from backgrounds of military, law enforcement, and security personnel worldwide. However, as situations recur from detail to detail and the field evolves, new words are developed and accepted. Included here are the most widely used terms and phrases that will help you "talk the talk."

Advance: A detail that goes ahead of the security team for the purpose of preparing for its arrival and ensuring its safety; a careful analysis of all areas and events that takes place prior to the team's arrival.

Armored Vehicle: A vehicle reinforced with protective metal and glass to withstand minor attacks.

Blending In: Providing protection without being obvious that such protection is being provided; becoming part of the corporate/family structure.

Body Armor: Protective gear generally used for high-threat assignments.

Bodyguard: Person or persons assigned to protect someone from harm. (See Executive and Personal Protection Specialists.)

Bugs/Bugging: Listening devices placed in appropriate places to gain information on a principal or company.

Bump: A tip or gratuity given as extra compensation in appreciation of an agent's service. (Generally considered standard practice among foreign clients, especially Arabs.)

Bump Frisk: Casually brushing against someone when he is suspected of carrying a concealed weapon, in order to feel for an object.

Call Sign: A code name used during radio transmissions.

Chase Car: Vehicle behind the principal's car.

Choke Points: Areas a principal must pass each day. Also, points where the client is most vulnerable to attack.

Client: The person being protected. (See Principal.)

Command Post: The center of operations of a detail.

Confidentiality: The ability to keep certain matters secret; an essential quality in all circles.

Corporate/Family Structure: Image of the personnel involved in routine operations of the company or family.

Countermeasures: Preventative actions taken in anticipation of an attack.

Covert Operations: Undercover activities; secret; clandestine.

Detail: Agents working as a team for the protection of a client. (Details vary in size depending upon the threat level.)

Discretion: Using judgment to act the best interest of the client.

Dress Down: The ability to change to a more casual appearance on short notice.

Dress Up: The ability to enhance your appearance on short notice.

Dress Code: A plan of action to alert another of one being in danger. Also, a specific word to be used as a signal in case of trouble.

Escape Route: A predetermined avenue to safety in case of an emergency during the course of a procession or during a scheduled event.

Escorts: Antiquated term for bodyguards.

ESI: Executive Security International. Executive protection school located near Aspen, Colorado.

Etiquette: Socially accepted behavior, mores, and mannerisms. Note: There are variations in every country.

Executive Protection Cocktail: A drink that appears to be alcoholic but isn't. Used at a cocktail party where the agent is blending in with other guests.

Executive Protection Specialist: (See Personal Protection Specialist.)

Formation: The manner of the detail; the positioning of the agents.

Government Sector: Security provided by agencies such as the Secret Service, military, states, and cities.

Gratuity: Extra compensation; a tip. (See Bump.)

Hardening Targets: A professional approach to protecting the client that involves the anticipation of any possible attack and the strengthening of all areas vulnerable to penetration.

Hardware: Weapons used on a detail.

High Profile: Image of the protective detail is obvious; maximum protection is necessary, i.e., a show of force.

High Threat Level: A possibility of imminent danger to the client, threats verified; maximum amount of protection necessary.

Hostage: A person taken against his or her will and held until demands are met.

Hostage Negotiator: A person skilled in negotiating for the release of hostages.

Identification Pins: Small pins worn on the lapel by

team members for identification purposes. Various colors are used at times to designate right of access to certain areas.

Inspection Mirror: A small mirror attached to a long handle which allows an agent to inspect under a vehicle for explosive or listening devices.

Intelligence: Information essential to a detail, generally obtained during a thorough advance.

Kidnapping: Abducting someone for ransom or other purposes; the main concern in protecting most clients, regardless of the threat level.

Kobetz and Associates: North Mountain Pines Institute Trainers of Personal Protection Specialists, and educators in numerous affiliated seminars. (See Nine Lives.)

KRI: Kidnap and ransom insurance.

Lead Car: Vehicle ahead of the principal's car; the vehicle at the head of the formation.

Letter Bomb: An envelope containing an explosive device that is activated upon breaking a seal when opening the paper.

Loose Cannon: An agent who does not work by the team concept. (There is no place on a detail for this type.)

Low Profile: Protective detail that blends into the corporate/family structure; the image of the detail is not obvious.

Low Threat Level: Low profile detail. No actual threats; protection necessary due to the status of the client.

Macho: Having an attitude of superiority.

Martial Arts: Defensive tactics invaluable for close maneuvers on details.

Medium Threat Level: Potential danger, but threats unverified; possible harassment calls or letters, but no overt action toward the client. Average detail assigned.

Mind-set: A person's attitude or frame of mind.

Mock Detail: An exercise for executive protection training simulating actual occurrences in public settings.

Nine Lives Associates: A fraternal organization of graduates of the North Mountain Pines Institute in Berryville, Virginia. (See Kobetz and Associates.)

Off-duty: The personal time of an agent still assigned to a detail; hours between shifts.

Off-the-air: The status of an agent who is in a position where it is inadvisable to respond to a radio; the radio is off.

Overt Operations: Actions that are not subdued or hidden and visually advise others of the detail's strength. Used in high-profile details.

Packing: A term used to determine whether one is carrying a weapon.

Panic Button: A device carried by or placed near a

client to be activated when immediate response to emergencies is needed.

Personal Protection Specialist: A professional bodyguard, educated and trained in above-average security duties. Synonymous with executive protection specialist.

Point-Man: The agent in front of a detail, protecting a client from the front.

Portfolio: A confidential case file on the client; includes all pertinent information and photos.

Principal: The person being protected, the client.

Private Sector: Private firms or individual agents providing protective services.

Professional: A security agent dedicated to his profession and educated in every aspect of it.

Profile: The image of the protective detail. (See High and Low Profile.)

Protectee: The client, the principal.

Protection: A service provided for the prevention of any harm to the clients, which includes harm from others or themselves, as well as general mishaps.

Protector: The agent, bodyguard. (See Executive and Personal Protection Specialist.)

Protocol: A set of rules or codes that dictates social behavior in official dealings and certain circles.

Ramrod: See Team Leader.

Risk Analysis: An evaluation of potential problems and the means and/or methods to avoid them.

Risk Factor: The degree of potential harm to an individual or association based upon circumstances or acts of others.

Roger: Acknowledgment in a radio transmission.

Routine: A set schedule; an activity performed in the same manner each time; a regular, unvaried procedure; a habit.

Sabotage: A deliberate act to cause damage to another's property; actions designed to render a detail ineffective.

Safe Room: A secure room easily accessible to the principal or his family in case of emergency. A room generally equipped with reinforced, bolted doors and separate phone line providing immediate communication with emergency services.

Search Room: A room utilized in training during advance checks for harmful or listening devices.

Stalker: One who constantly pursues the attention or affection of another against his or her will; one who follows another in a threatening manner.

Straphangers: People who want to always be around the principal for the benefits; those who want a free ride.

Surveillance: The act of watching and monitoring the activities of another.

Sweep: A structured method of checking an area for

explosive devices or other problems; an electronic means of surveying a room for "bugs," i.e., listening devices.

Tail Man: Agent to the rear of a detail, protecting against attacks from the back.

Take Down: The moment the detail begins; time of arrival of the vehicle, e.g., airplane.

Team: Agents working together to protect a principal. (See Detail.)

Team Leader: The agent in charge of the team. The one who coordinates the assignments of the agents and movements of the principal.

Terrorism: Terror created by others that is directed at a principal for the purpose of causing major problems to the principal and his or her family or business, and that would directly or indirectly benefit those causing the problems.

Terrorist: A person who willfully plans or commits acts for the purpose of causing terror to others.

Threat Level: The degree of a threat to a principal, and the amount of potential danger the client faces.

Thumb Peel: A specific method of disengaging a firm handshake with the principal when the other party holds on too long.

Vance International: Trainers and providers of high quality personnel for executive protection throughout the world, based in Oakton, Virginia.

Visual Protective Area: The area assigned to each

agent in a detail that provides protection with a minimum amount of head movement.

Wheels Up: The scheduled time for a plane to take
off; the end of a detail.

Wrangler: See Team Leader.

Appendix C

Recommended Reading

This section includes a bibliography of many fine works relating to the protection field. While the focus is on nonfiction and special articles, several works of fiction are included. Throughout the book there has been an emphasis on continuing education. Therefore, it is extremely important to have a working knowledge of the literary contributions to our profession. This is only a small selection of the numerous books and articles available, each of which I have reviewed. I consider these publications valuable educational resources in learning from the experiences of others. The fact that some publications are not on this list does not reflect a negative opinion of such works, but merely a lack of opportunity on my part to review them.

Whether you read for pure education or merely to escape reality, the knowledge attained through publications, coupled with your own experiences and enhanced by the actual teachings of others, will prove to be invaluable resources in your pursuit of professionalism.

Anti-Defamation League of B'nai B'rith. *Extremism on the Right.* New York: 1983.

Baldridge, Letitia. *Amy Vanderbilt's Everyday Etiquette.* New York: Bantam Books, 1980.

Bamford, James. *The Puzzle Palace.* New York: Penguin Books, 1982.

Barron, John. *KGB Today: The Hidden Hand.* New York: Reader's Digest Press, 1983.

Bodansky, Yossef. *Target America.* New York: S.P.I. Books, 1993.

_____. *Terror.* New York: S.P.I. Books, 1994.

Bremer, Arthur H. *An Assassin's Diary.* New York: Harper & Row, 1972.

Brigham Young University. *Culturgrams.* (Brief publications relating to over 100 areas of the world, providing material on nations, the people, their customs, and other general information.)

Brown, Harold. *Thinking about National Security.* New York: Hearst Books, 1983.

Carlson, Kurt. *One American Must Die.* New York: Congdon & Weed, Inc., 1986.

Chafets, Ze'ev. *Double Vision.* New York: William Morrow & Company, 1985.

Collins, Larry, and Dominique Lapierre. *The Fifth Horseman.* New York: Avon Books, 1980.

Cooper, H.H.A. *On Assassination.* Boulder, Colorado: Paladin Press, 1984.

Cooper, H.H.A., and Lawrence J. Redlinger. *Catching Spies.* Boulder, Colorado: Paladin Press, 1988.

_____. *Making Spies.* Boulder, Colorado: Paladin Press, 1986.

Copeland, Lennie, and Lewis Griggs. *Going International.* New York: Random House, Inc., 1985.

Cuddihy, Kathy. *Saudi Customs and Etiquette.* Hong Kong: Peregrine Publishing, 1990.

Dobson, Christopher, and Ronald Payne. *The Never Ending War: Terrorism in the '80s.* New York:

Facts on File, 1987.

Eisenberg, Dennis, Uri Dan, and Eli Landau. *The Mossad*. New York: Signet Books, 1978.

Elhanan, Paul. *Keep 'em Alive: The Bodyguard's Trade*. Boulder, Colorado: Paladin Press, 1985.

Emerson, Ryan Quade. *U.S. Terrorists – Radicals – Revolutionaries*. Purcellville, Virginia: The Zeus Group, 1987.

_____. *Who's Who in Terrorism*. Purcellville, Virginia: The Zeus Group, 1987.

Emerson, Steven A. and Christina Del Sesto. *Terrorist*. New York: Villard Books, 1991.

Farrell, William R. *Blood and Rage*. Lexington, Massachusetts: Lexington Books, 1990.

Flynn, Joe B. *The Design of Executive Protection Systems*. Springfield, Illinois: Charles C. Thomas, Pub., Bannerstone House, 1979.

Freemantle, Brian. *KGB*. New York: Holt, Rinehart, and Winston, 1982.

Friedman, Thomas L. *From Beirut to Jerusalem*. New York: Farrar, Straus, Giroux, 1989.

Goddard, Kenneth. *Balefire*. New York: Bantam Books, 1983.

Gregory, Harry. *Khadafy*. New York: Paper Jacks, Ltd., 1986.

Hall, Sam. *Counter-Terrorist*. New York: Donald I. Fine, Inc., 1987.

Hoffman, Bruce. *Recent Trends and Future Prospects of Terrorism in the United States*. Santa Monica, California: Rand Corporation, 1988.

"How Iran's Terrorists Operate." *U.S. News & World Report* (6 March 1989): 20-25.

Jacobson, David. *Hostage*. New York: Donald I. Fine, Inc., 1991.

Jenkins, Brian Michael. *Terrorism and Personal Protection*. Stoneham, Massachusetts: Butterworth Publishers, 1985.

Jonas, George. *Vengeance.* New York: Bantam Books, Simon & Schuster, 1984.

Jones, Jack. *Let Me Take You Down.* New York: Villard Books, Random House, Inc., 1992.

Kobetz, Richard W. *Providing Executive Protection.* Berryville, Virginia: Executive Protection Institute, 1991.

Kobetz, Richard W., and H.H.A. Cooper. *Target Terrorism: Providing Protective Services.* Gaitherburg, Maryland: International Association of Chiefs of Police, 1978.

Lacey, Robert. *The Kingdom: Arabia & the House of Sa'ud.* New York: Avon Books, 1981.

Laffin, John. *The PLO Connections.* London: Corgi Books Transworld Publishers, Ltd., Century House, 1982.

Laqueur, Walter, and Yonah Alexander. *The Terrorism Reader.* New York: Meridian, NAL Penguin, Inc., 1978.

Lippman, Thomas W. *Understanding Islam.* New York: Mentor New American Library, 1982.

Mattman, Jurg W. *Executive Security and Safety.* Fullerton, California: J. Mattman Security, 1982.

McCarthy, Dennis V. *Protecting the President.* New York: William Morrow & Company, 1985.

Melman, Yossi. *The Master Terrorist.* New York: Avon Books, 1986.

Metcalf, Geoffrey. *The Terrorist Killers.* New York: Critic's Choice, 1988.

Michaud, John. "The Feminine Touch." *Police Product News* (December 1985): 30.

Mills, James. *The Underground Empire.* New York: Dell Publishing Company, Inc., 1986.

Molloy, John T. *New Dress for Success.* New York: Warner Books, Inc.,1990.

Momboisse, Raymond M. *Riots, Revolts and Insurrections.* Springfield, Illinois: Charles C. Thomas, Pub., Bannerstone House, 1967.

Moore, Larry R. "Women on the Dark Side." *Security Management Magazine* (July 1986): 47-50.

Morrell, David. *The Fifth Profession*. New York: Warner Books, Inc.,1990.

Netanyahu, Benjamin. *Terrorism: How the West Can Win*. New York: Farrar, Straus, Giroux, 1986.

Ostrovsky, Victor, and Claire Hoy. *By Way of Deception*. New York: St.Martin's Press, 1990.

Pollack, J.C. *Threat Case*. New York, Delacorte Press, 1991.

Rapp, Burt. *Bodyguarding: A Complete Manual*. Port Townsend, Washington: Loompanics Unlimited, 1988.

Raviv, Dan, and Yossi Melman. *Every Spy a Prince*. Boston: Houghton Mifflin Company, 1990.

Reber, Jan, and Paul Shaw. *Executive Protection Manual*. Schiller Park, Illinois: MTI Teleprograms, Inc., 1976.

Rivers, Gayle. *The Killing House*. New York: G.P. Putnam's Sons, 1988.

_____. *The Specialist*. Briarcliff Manor, New York: Stein and Day Publishers, Scarborough House, 1985.

_____. *The War against the Terrorists*. Briarcliff Manor, New York: Stein and Day Publishers, Scarborough House, 1986.

Scotti, Anthony J. *Executive Safety and International Terrorism*. Englewood Cliffs, New Jersey: Prentice-Hall, Inc., 1986.

Seale, Patrick. *Abu Nidal: A Gun for Hire*. New York: Random House, Inc., 1992.

Siljander, Raymond P. *Terrorist Attacks*. Springfield, Illinois: Charles C. Thomas, Pub., Bannerstone House, 1980.

Smith, Bradley, and Gus Stevens. *The Emergency Book: You Can Save a Life!* New York: Simon & Schuster, 1978.

Sterling, Claire. *The Terror Network*. New York: Holt, Rinehart and Winston, 1981.

_____. *The Time of the Assassins*. New York: Holt, Rinehart and Winston, 1983.

Taheri, Amir. *Holy Terror*. Bethesda, Maryland: Adler

and Adler Publishers, Inc., 1987.

Thompson, Leroy. *Dead Clients Don't Pay*. Boulder, Colorado: Paladin Press, Inc., 1984.

Tinnin, David B. *The Hit Team*. Boston: Little, Brown and Company, 1976.